Love One Another
Reclaiming the Christian Distinctive

Michael L Chiavone

Love One Another: Reclaiming the Christian Distinctive

Copyright © 2016. All rights reserved. Except for brief quotations in critical articles or reviews, no part of this book may be reproduced in any manner without written permission from the author.

ISBN-13: 978-1544869384
ISBN-10: 154486938X

Scripture quotations, aside from those translated by the author, are taken from the King James Version.

To all my brothers and sisters in Christ

Contents

Preface vi

"God Loved the World this Way" 1

"Herein is Love" 11

"On this Hangs All the Law and the Prophets" 21

"No Respect of Persons" 33

"I Will Go Down Now, and See" 49

"If Thy Brother Shall Trespass" 67

"Leave There Thy Gift Before the Altar" 79

"More than 120,000 Persons" 89

"Speaking the Truth in Love" 97

"Abhor Evil, Cleave to Good" 108

"Love is ..." 118

Bibliography 126

Preface

On the night before he was executed, Jesus ate the Last Supper with his disciples. After the supper, he conducted himself as a servant and washed their feet. After this, he told them that they should serve one another as he had served them. He told the disciples that he would be leaving them and then said, "A new commandment I give unto you, that ye love one another; as I have loved you, that ye also love one another. By this shall all men know that ye are my disciples, if ye have love one to another" (John 13:34-35).[1] Jesus gave to his disciples a command and a sign. They were to love one another as he has loved them and, when they did so, all would know that they were his disciples.

It is interesting that Jesus calls this a new commandment. He has been teaching about the importance of loving others, as commanded in Lev 19:18, during his ministry. He tells the story of the Good Samaritan in response to a question about this commandment (Luke 10:27-37). It is this command, to love one's neighbor as oneself, which he calls second only to loving God (Matt 22:39). How then, if one is to love one's neighbor, can the command to the disciples to love one another be a new command?

The answer must lie in the two differences between John 13:34 and Lev 19:18. One is the change of the people involved. Leviticus had commanded the Israelites to love their

---

[1] Unless otherwise noted, all Bible quotations are from the *King James Version* or are the author's own translation.

neighbors. Jesus commands his followers to love each other. The other is the change of the manner of love. Leviticus had commanded the Israelites to love others as themselves. Jesus commands his disciples to love as he has loved them. His disciples are to love one another in a new way. Not only should they love each other as themselves, but they should love each other in the way that he, Christ, loves them. That way, as he knows, is a love that sacrifices even unto death. While loving one's neighbor as oneself suggests a balance, an equality, between one's concern for others and one's concern for self, to love as Christ loves involves putting others above self. These distinctions, a higher manner of love shared among a smaller selection of people, would serve as a sign to distinguish them from the rest of the world. Christians would still love others, of course, but the shared love among them would be a manifest distinguishing characteristic.

Have twenty-first century American Christians really fulfilled this command and manifested this distinctive? I have heard comments from believers that make me fear that we have not. We have all, I think, heard statements like the following spoken by Christians. "Christians are the only army who shoot their own wounded." "I have never been treated as badly by the world as I have been by Christians." As James says, "My brethren, these things ought not so to be" (James 3:10).

This text is written to try to right this wrong. Christians should be identifiable by their Christ-like love for one another. Identifiable. Recognizable. The love believers have for one another should be part of that light which so shines before other men that they see the way Christians treat one another and, in their response, glorify the Father in heaven (Matt 5:16). This is a heady requirement. It suggests that Christian love will be visible. It will manifest itself in ways that go beyond good feelings and pleasant dispositions. It will be a distinctive.

To begin with, we will consider the basic character of the love Jesus has in mind and basic guidelines for putting it into practice. Then, we will look at how that love connects to the rest of the commands in the Bible. In the chapters that follow, we will consider how to put that love into practice in several very common, very practical areas of our daily Christian lives.

Before getting to the subject at hand, I would like to make a few comments about my word usage. First, when writing of God in Himself, I have chosen to capitalize pronouns both to follow the tradition of such respectful formatting and to clarify sentences in which both God and a human person are possible antecedents. This is the case whether speaking of the Trinity, God the Father, God the Son, or God the Spirit. Second, when writing of God the Son in the Incarnation, in His own humanity as the man Christ Jesus, I have chosen to not capitalize pronouns used of him in that state. This is not to deny Jesus' true deity, but to recognize his true humanity. The Son, He, condescended to be like us, and took on His own full humanity when He became him, the man Christ Jesus. Third, I have mixed using masculine and feminine generics in the work, and mixed male and female examples in the text. I have not consciously tried to connect either gender or sex to the examples raised, unless stated or obviously otherwise, so nothing should be read into the gender or sex used for a particular example unless ethics related to the sexes are specifically in view. Fourth, I have, for the sake of readability and "tone," often employed first person plurals, we, us, and our, to include myself in collective referrals to Christians. I beg the reader's indulgence of this convention, as I know that an individual reader may not always be included in the "we" who "do" or "do not do" a certain thing. No false judgment is intended with such language.

"God Loved the World this Way"

It is fitting to begin a consideration of love with an examination of John 3:16, "For God so loved the world, that He gave his only begotten Son, that whosoever believeth in him should not perish, but have everlasting life." This verse, or at least its citation, is probably the best known in contemporary America. One sees it referenced on placards in all sorts of venues the world over. It is the "go to" verse when thinking about the Christian idea of God's love.

As common as the verse's citation is, however, is a misunderstanding of a word in the verse, the word, "so." Often, people automatically insert a "much" after the "so," as in, "God loved the world so much that He gave." This makes the verse about the quantity or intensity of God's love. However, this is not what "so" means in such a usage. If you say, "I think so," you mean, "I think that way," not, "I think so much." "Are the Steelers going to win the Superbowl this year?" "I think so." I think that way. Similar expressions are, "Like so," and, "Just so." "So" is used to describe a manner or type; in this case, it is about the manner or type of God's love.[2] John 3:16 presents the character, the manner, of God's love.

---

[2] For those interested, the Greek here is ουτως. It is the adverbial form of the demonstrative pronoun, equivalent in form to the English non-word, "thisly." It is not used in Scripture when we have an English translation of "so much," as in Matt 15:33 or Mark 7:36. It is used to in places like Matt 13:49 and Mark 4:26 to mean "like this."

God loves the world "so"; this way, and not some other way.

In one sense, it makes little difference whether John 3:16 is about the amount or manner of God's love. The important part is what comes after, what God has done. But if we are going to imitate this sort of love, it can make a difference in how we think. If love is a matter of quantity, if it can be counted up and weighed, then people can claim to love, but not enough. And they do. Does a friend need help with something? "I love you man, but not that much." Is a marriage in trouble? "I love my wife, but not enough to put up with that." If love is a scale, one can love, love like God loves, but not enough to do what is right, and still call it love. But if we focus on love as a manner, as a type of love, it is harder to maintain that charade. We either love like God loves, the way He loves, or we do not. Our imitation is not about loving as much as God loves, as if we could. It is about loving the way that He loves. This is what John 3:16 tells us. This is the way that God loves the world. That way is characterized by several features.

First and foremost, God's love gives. It is not a love of simple goodwill, as if God were a well-wisher who hoped nothing bad, and perhaps something good, befell the world, the object of His love. It is not a love that just watches, much less takes from, the one loved. It is a love that thus moves in one direction, from a giver through his gift to the recipient.

Second, God's love gives something precious. Certainly, giving away anything can be generous. But we all recognize that there are some things it is easy to give away. For example, most people will not begrudge anyone a Tic-Tac. The more valuable something is to the one who holds it, the more generous we consider him if he is willing to give it away. The man who "would give you the shirt off his back" is commended not just because he gives, but because he gives something he apparently values enough to be wearing right now, and presumably leaves himself without any shirt for the moment. He gives up more than just an object; he gives up his place of superiority over the one who has no shirt. He humbles himself as well; walking around in public without a shirt is usually tacky at best.

God goes far beyond even this in His love. He gives up His Son unto death. The God of the Bible is creator and possessor of heaven and earth. There is nothing He might give away which He could not immediately replace except for a Person of the Godhead. As God Himself says, He has no need for what men might give Him; He has cattle on a thousand hills (Psalm 50:7-12). When David sought to forestall God's judgement upon Jerusalem, he offered sacrifices before the Lord on the threshing floor of Araunah. Araunah was willing to give David whatever he wanted, but David refused, unwilling to offer to God what cost him nothing (2 Sam 24:24). God's love for the world is of such a kind that He gives something valuable beyond price, the life of His only begotten Son.

This truth is so familiar it can be difficult to consider as those who first heard it must have. But stop for a moment and think, What would you think of a human who gave up his son to certain death? If you are a parent, ask yourself, For what would you give up your child to certain death? Such a decision is almost unthinkable. The closest parallel we might pose would be the parents who support a child's decision to serve in the military. But there death is not certain, though it is a risk. And even though it is a risk, and not certain, do we not recognize the great love such parents must have for their country? Would we not, if the country were unworthy of such love, fault such parents for their willingness to give up their child for an unworthy object? Yet this is what God has done. This is His love. For a world that is His enemy, He gives His Son up to certain death.

Third, God's love seeks the good of the one loved. Here, God's love seeks to provide a way of escape so that the world might not perish but that instead believers might gain everlasting life. God's love does not seek His own good, but the good of the object of love. All God does in this verse is love and give; He does not gain. Indeed, being the self-existent, all-sufficient creator of all things other than Himself, God cannot gain. His love for man is entirely and inherently selfless, unless we would count the pleasure any of us feels in simply doing what we choose to do as selfish.

Fourth, God's love seeks the highest good of the one loved. When Jesus walked the earth, many people came to him with requests and real needs. And, he met many of those needs. He healed the sick, cast out demons, and fed the needy. But God's love is such that healing the sick or multiplying the loaves does not adequately characterize it. It is His action to provide for mankind's ultimate good, eternal life, which conveys the character of His love. Conversely, Paul will later make clear that self-sacrificial actions, even extreme ones, are pointless if the genuine good of others is not their end: "If I give my body to be burned, but do not love, it is worthless" (1 Cor 13:3).

And, in order to provide for that ultimate good, God at times denied people the lesser things, even good things, they wanted. There was a time when the people who followed Jesus would have made him an earthly king by force. Certainly, this would have been good for those people; imagine if Jesus were ruling over America, or even the whole world, today. Imagine the peace, the righteousness, the goodness, and the bounty. But Jesus avoided this (John 6:15). He would not be made king only to bring these people temporal goods. When the multitude sought him to provide an ongoing source of food (John 6:34), he confronted them over the real question of their need for salvation unto eternal life (John 6:47-48), though he knew it would result in many of his followers withdrawing from him (John 6:64, 66). He set aside their lesser benefit to point them to their need for a greater one.

God's love thus might be defined, "A desire for the highest good of another that causes one to act, even at cost to himself, to bring about that good." This is the way God loved the world. And, it is the way that Jesus loved us. As he said, "Greater love has no man than this, that a man lay down his life for his friends" (John 15:13). His willing choice to die for man, a choice which he could have made otherwise (Matt 26:53), is rooted in and is exemplary of that same kind of love.

So, when Jesus says to his disciples, "A new commandment I give unto you, that ye love one another; as I have loved you, that ye also love one another. By this shall all men know that ye are my disciples, if ye have love one to another" (John 13:34), he is commanding his followers to love one another in just this sort of way. He is not commanding them to love one another according to the standards of their society, according to the wisdom of their wise men, or according to their family traditions. It is a command to do as he has done. It is a command to consider the good, the highest good, of each other and then seek to implement it, even at the cost of death. As we deal with each other in the church, in the community, in the home, in the workplace, or wherever we see one another, our minds should be on, What is best for you?

It is an understatement to say that this is not our natural way of thinking. It is natural to think, What is best for me? We are selfish creatures. The Bible takes for granted that people will seek their own good. The command of Lev 19:18, which Jesus will later say is the second greatest commandment and the basis for the Law (Matt 22:39-40), is that man love his neighbor as himself. This command has little meaning or value if one is not already loving himself, not already seeking his own good. That default approach to life need not be commanded. It is natural.

If pure selfishness is the natural way of thinking, how is it that many Christians perceive the world to treat them better than other believers do? Should not natural selfishness run rampant in the world? No, because the world, at least the American world, has come to understand that most people best satisfy their selfishness through trade, through meeting the desires of others. If I am sitting across a counter from a worldly business owner, for example, he wants what is best for him. But he believes, if only subconsciously, that the way for him to get what is best for him is to see that I get what I want. If I am a worker and he desires my labor, he knows he cannot get it unless he pays me and cannot keep it unless he pays me enough to keep me from seeking employment elsewhere. If he can get more benefit out of me than it costs him to employ me, he is glad to pay me because he has a net gain; he profits. If I am a customer and he desires my cash, he knows he cannot get it unless he gives me something I want. None of this is said, by the way, to impugn this way of thinking or to deny that there are forms of altruism in the world. It is only to point out why many Christians, when interacting with the world, encounter treatment that seems to be seeking their best even when no moral command from God demands that it be so.

How then, do many Christians fail so completely to love one another that a world which lacks such a command better fulfills it than they do? The answer, I would suggest, is that they become accustomed to the idea of being the object of love, rather than the lover. If God has loved me in this way, should not everyone else? Since God has commanded other Christians to love me, should they not do so? Am I not, in a sense, entitled to the love of other Christians? Do they not owe that love to me? Of course they do. And, since they do, I can presume that they are quite happy to think of me first and seek my best, even at expense to themselves.

I once worked at a small business which provided a face-to-face service to its customers and involved billing rather than payment on delivery of services. The owner and manager was not a Christian, but my supervisor was and had been a living testimony before him for years. I was shamed to hear what she told me one day. She said to me that the owner occasionally received notes in lieu of payment which expressed the sentiment, "We are Christians and we trust you are too. We cannot pay you this month and assume that, as a Christian, you will overlook our not paying you. God bless." In this thinking, the commandment and character of Christ's love has been totally reversed. This is farther from the command than even the natural selfishness of the world. Jesus' command is, "Seek the good of others at expense to yourself." The world's thinking is, "Seek your good." But this pseudo-Christian thinking is, "Seek your good at expense to others." I write "pseudo-Christian," but anti-Christian is more accurate; it is antithetical to the command of Christ. And, in this case, it was a severe hindrance to the progress of the gospel in the life of a man who needed Christ.

It is, however, shockingly common. I regularly receive, in my interactions with other Christians, demands for consideration which show no concern whatsoever for me. Since I have encountered this thinking in seminaries, where Christian leaders are being trained, I can only assume that it is spread out in churches as well. Of course, there are times when we have needs and it is right for us to turn to other Christians to see God meet those needs, but we should guard against turning God's command to us that we love into an expectation that we be loved. God's love is about giving, not gain. If we are to love as He loves, we need to be the same.

So, as we seek to recapture God's command to love one another, our focus cannot be on getting others to love us or acting with the expectation that they will. Even as I write this,

I consider that my goal as I think through this command needs to be to implement it in my life, not benefit from others implementing it in theirs. We need to think of the command as calling us to commit to the following. "I will love other Christians. I will seek their good, their highest good, and try to bring it about even at expense to myself."

Some may balk at this. It is truly a large commitment. Some may be concerned that this will allow them to be taken advantage of, that it will result in them being at everyone's beck and call, effectively everyone's servant. To that three things must be said. First, it should be noted that Jesus did not look at this last as a bad thing: "Whosoever of you will be the chiefest, shall be servant of all" (Mark 10:44). Second, as will be discussed more later, the character of love does not mean doing everything everyone wants you to do. It does not mean being "a doormat." Finally, it should be recognized that this is a command of Christ, that I love other Christians. It is not an optional objective for bonus points. Violating this command is as much a sin as is committing adultery or murder. The next chapter will continue to explore what it means to love as God loves.

Reflection Questions
1. John 3:16 characterizes God's love as having a certain quality, rather than a certain quantity. What difference does this make in how we think of God's love?

2. Of the things you have sacrificed in love for others, what was the most difficult or painful to sacrifice?

3. Of the things you might be called upon to sacrifice in love for others, what would be the most difficult?

"Herein is Love"

In 1 John 4:10-11, John writes, "Herein is love, not that we loved God, but that he loved us, and sent his Son to be the propitiation for our sins. Beloved, if God so loved us, we ought also to love one another." In John 3:16, Jesus describes God's love for the world. Here in 1 John 4:10, John makes that description the definition of love. Jesus says, "God loves like this." John says, "God's love defines love." It is in the sacrificial love of God for the world that love is seen, nowhere else.

The thing to note about this love is its unilateral nature. This is not a two-sided arrangement. While John does recognize that believers love God in v. 19, he is clear in v. 10 that this response of love is not a necessary component in true love. God loves us. We love him. The two sentences refer to distinct realities, not a singular love relationship with two cooperating participants.

In contemporary American culture, love is still recognized as a virtue. However, the definition of that love is usually changed from the picture John presents, in emphasis if not in nature. Sometimes, love is shifted to mean a reciprocal relationship. Other times, love is focused on emotions. Both of these redefinitions make it difficult for believers to obey the command to love one another.

Love and Relationship

The move to view love as a reciprocal relationship is rooted in our human experience. The loving relationships we enjoy most are those in which we both love and are loved. Within marriage, a spouse may go through a time when she does not perceive that she is being loved. She quite reasonably considers this less than ideal. Parents love their infant children and take care of them, but what parents do not enjoy it when their children make the transition to showing affection for them as well? We look eagerly for the earliest hint that a child is responding to us: a flash of a smile, a bit of a giggle, the clutch of a finger. We take the first sounds babbling children make and use them as the names for parents so that we can say, "He said mama!" or "papa!" or "dada!" It is not unusual to read authors discuss love as if a reciprocal relationship of mutual love is the only form of love worthy of the name. Even God is being brought down to this human level; movements such as open theism revise theology to view the relationship between God and humans as a reciprocal love between adult humans.

But this is not how John defines normative love. He specifically excludes the human response to God's love from the definition. God loving us is love. And it is essential that believers seeking to obey the command to love one another recognize that their responsibility is to love, not to form mutually loving reciprocal relationships among equals. While this may be where we want love to go in both the home and the church, this is not what the command means. And, viewing the command to love as the command to form mutually loving relationships leads to problems.

First, viewing love in reciprocal terms often leads people to wait to be loved before they love. If I will love you when you start loving me, and you will love me when I start loving you, neither of us will ever love the other. As a parallel, the Bible commands husbands to love their wives and wives to submit to their husbands. Many a marriage has suffered because the spouses viewed these commands as conditional on one another. He waited for her to submit before he loved, and she waited for him to love before she would submit. In the meantime, both were miserable. Thinking of love primarily or solely in terms of a mutual relationship has similar results.

Imagine if God's love operated in this way, rather than in the way we see it operate in John 3:16. God sits enthroned on high and looks down at humanity and says, "If they will love Me, I will send a savior." Humanity looks up and perhaps says, "If God would send a savior, I would love Him." How tragic that would have been. But this is not how God's love worked. While we were yet sinners, while we were enemies, Christ died for us.

Second, viewing love in reciprocal terms leads to frustration even if one is willing to take the first step. Imagine two men in a church, Tim and Joe. Tim wants to love Joe; that is, he wants to establish a mutual, reciprocal relationship with Joe. He believes, though, that he is obligated to take the first step, and so he does, mowing Joe's lawn while Joe is out of town. Over the next several months, Tim does several more generous things for Joe, but nothing comes of it. Joe never calls Tim up to get together or returns a favor in kind. Tim is likely to be frustrated and look at his efforts as failures because he has not established that mutual relationship. He tried to love, but failed.

But John 3:16 says God's love is precisely not this. The human response mentioned in the verse, believing, has no bearing on God's love either way. It affects only the fate of the one who believes. God loves, acts, sends. Man believes to his own benefit or disbelieves to his own loss. God's role is solely to love. Again, the relationship is the desired, ideal result. Those who receive Christ become children of God (John 1:12). But God's love, properly understood, is His giving, not the response to that giving. So, when love is properly understood it is clear that Tim has not failed. Tim has desired Joe's good and acted to bring it about at expense to himself. Each time he has done this, he has successfully loved Joe, regardless of Joe's response.

A group of youth participated in the World Changers ministry of the Southern Baptist Convention, in which young people help restore and renovate homes for those who cannot afford to do so. One activity this group engaged in after their main work was called "Light Bulb Visitation." The youth took light bulbs around the neighborhood in boxes which were effectively gospel tracts. They gave people light bulbs and shared the light and love of Christ in the neighborhoods in which they were working. Upon returning to their home churches, they reported on the whole experience, and many emphasized the "Light Bulb Visitation" as a highlight. After the presentation I was talking to one of the youth, whom we will call William, who seemed down about it. I asked him what the problem was. He said that his experience had been different from what everyone else had described. He had been yelled at, had doors shut on him, etc. It sounded like no one had responded even pleasantly to William, and he felt as if he had failed. So, I asked him about what he had done. Had he yelled at anyone? Cursed them? Given up? If not, he had done as well as anyone else, perhaps better. He had loved. The responses he received were not his responsibility and no reflection on him at all.

Love and Feelings

The move to view love as primarily an emotional experience is also rooted in our experience. The emotional attachments we form in our loving relationships are an integral part of those relationships, both as causes and effects. The marriage bond, in our culture, usually forms as a consequence of a prior emotional connection. We "fall in love" and then make a commitment to love. Within the context of passionate, intimate love we conceive children, whom we love as well. At the same time, the shared experiences and personal closeness of the family relationship strengthen and reinforce the emotional bonds of love within the family. Our daily experience of familial love, which is our primary frame of reference for viewing love, is a comprehensive package of commitment, emotions, and interactive relationships. It is difficult to step out of that as we seek to love one another.

Yet it is important to recognize that the biblical picture of God's love for man is not presented in these terms. Paul says it was not when we were loved family members, but "when we were enemies," that "we were reconciled to God by the death of his Son" (Rom 5:10). God's love for man does not begin while men are close, intimate members of His household. While the story of the prodigal son is about a family, it is about a family in which personal, emotional closeness is frayed, if not broken. Jesus presents the invitation to God's kingdom as an invitation not to the friends of the host, but to strangers, to the poor, maimed, halt, and blind, who are compelled to come to a feast to which they were not originally invited (Luke 14:16-24). God's love is not reserved for His close companions.

Nor can Jesus' commands to love be understood to reflect a romantic or familial view of emotional love. Jesus says, "Love your enemies, and do good to them which hate you . . . love ye your enemies, and do good, and lend, hoping for nothing again" (Luke 6:27, 35). Jokes about black sheep and relatives aside, an enemy is certainly not one with whom you have a close emotional connection. So, it is important to separate our common experience of love, in which loving actions, personal intimacy, shared experiences, and reciprocal relationships are bound together, from the core of Jesus' command to love. If we do not, problems are certain to follow.

The first occurs when believers judge their love based upon their feelings of love. Some believers attempt to conjure up feelings of love for those whom they do not love before taking action. Usually, these efforts are in vain. We experience much of emotion as autonomic, that is, involuntary, responses. Feelings of love usually develop as a result of shared exciting experiences. Other believers take action without the feelings of love, and instead feel silly, guilty, or even hypocritical for doing so. Believing the core of the command to love is to feel, they believe they are just "going through the motions," and that this cannot be right. Many times these feelings of guilt or disingenuousness eventually result in them giving up on loving. Finally, there are those who take action expecting feelings of love to follow. Sometimes they do, of course, but sometimes, as in William's case above, the responses to our efforts to love just leave us feeling worse.

The second problem that occurs if emotional love is the focus of the command to love is when believers stop at feeling love. If the command to love is to feel love and I feel love, my work here is done. This approach is manifested in the person who thinks that a general expression of goodwill, that greeting everyone as "brother," and that genuinely feeling sympathy with those who suffer exhausts his responsibility. Now certainly, such a person is often in a unique position to effectively love. But his feelings do not fulfill the commands of Jesus. As James writes, "If a brother or sister be naked, and destitute of daily food, and one of you say unto them, Depart in peace, be ye warmed and filled; notwithstanding ye give them not those things which are needful to the body; what doth it profit? Even so faith, if it hath not works, is dead, being alone" (James 2:15-17). While his discussion is explicitly about faith, it seems quite obvious that love, even more than faith, is dead without works. In the last chapter, love was defined as a desire that leads to action. To consider the task of loving complete at the stage of good feelings or generic hope that things go well for another is to leave it incomplete. Indeed, there is a sense in which John 3:16 presents God's love as the act of giving itself. It is only other passages, such as Isa 63:9, in which "in love" is seen to describe an act of God, which encourage us to distinguish between love and loving action. But that distinction cannot be separation. True love acts.

None of this should be taken to mean that love that fulfills Christ's command cannot result in reciprocal relationships or emotional attachments. It often does. Christians are adopted into a filial relationship with God the Father through His loving sending of the Son (Gal 4:4-5). But this is a consequence we can hope follows our love for each other; it is neither the ground of nor the test for that love.

"You Will Be with Me in Paradise"

On the Cross, as he is experiencing the agony of crucifixion unblunted by the drink offered him, Christ hears railing from all around. The people cry for his blood. The rulers scoff at him. The soldiers mock him. Even two wicked men crucified with him "cast the same in his teeth" (Matt 27:44). But at some point one of them, recognizing the innocence of the Son of God and trusting that God will vindicate him, appeals to him saying, "Lord, remember me when you come into your kingdom" (Luke 23:42). Jesus is in agony, having been scourged and crucified. He suffers the emotional pain of facing his impending unjust death. And now a man is asking him for a favor.

Think on that. Jesus has been scourged, the flesh of his back laid open with a whip. The weight of his body now hangs upon three nails through his hands and feet, bone on iron. And now someone is asking him for something. They are not friends; as far as we know, this man has never seen Jesus before. This man is not doing anything for Jesus and indeed can offer him nothing. Yet Jesus responds to this man, assuring him that he will enjoy the blessed redemption which Jesus is securing him by his death: "Verily I say unto you, Today shall you be with me in paradise." This is love. This defines love. When we offer favors to people who were strangers that morning and mocking us an hour ago, we love. We may hope for better things after, but they are exactly that: after.

The type of love God shows to us and demands of the followers of Jesus is this kind of love. It is not defined by the feelings we feel or the results we see. It is defined by selfless willing giving for the highest good of another. Understanding love this way makes it possible to love. It also implies that it will often be painful or difficult, but for those who have been indwelt by Christ's Spirit, it will at least be possible.

Reflection Questions
1. Can you think of a time when your efforts to love were hindered because you were looking to feel a certain way or receive a certain response?

2. As noted above, "God loving us is love." Does any part of you bristle at this idea? Why or why not?

3. When you think of love in terms of self-costing action, what would you say is the most loving thing you have ever done? Is it different from the most loving thing you have done if love is defined as an emotional relationship?

"On This Hangs All the Law and the Prophets"

It is fairly common in contemporary America, and even contemporary American Christianity, for people to put love and law in opposition to one another. Joseph Fletcher in his *Situation Ethics*[3] articulated the position that no law or set of laws could adequately answer ethical dilemmas. Instead, one should do what is loving in any particular situation, even if that loving act was something that, in other situations or according to specific moral laws, would be clearly immoral. People speak of "loving" as opposed to "being legalistic." Recently, both people who desire legal sanction for their lifestyles of homosexual deviancy and people who enter the country illegally have been presented as sympathetic objects because they are acting out of love. In the face of love, what can law matter?

Jesus, however, never set the command to love over against following the laws of God. He says, "If you love me, keep my commandments" (John 14:15), and, "He that has my commandments, and keepeth them, he it is that loves me" (John 14:21). Lest one should think keeping Christ's commandments is fundamentally different from obeying the Bible in general, Christ says that "all the law and prophets" hang on the twin commands to love God and to love one's neighbor (Matt 22:40). Loving is not disconnected from the other commands of God.

---

[3](Philadelphia: Westminster, 1966).

The New Testament authors continue to make this connection. Paul, after speaking of the liberty believers have in Christ, charges them to use their liberty not "for an occasion to the flesh, but by love serve one another. For all the law is fulfilled in one word, *even* in this; Thou shalt love thy neighbor as thyself" (Gal 5:13-14). After listing those of the Ten Commandments relevant to how men treat each other, Paul states that all of them, and "any other commandment . . . is briefly comprehended in this saying, namely, Thou shalt love thy neighbour as thyself" (Rom 13:8-9). John says, quite simply and directly, "And this is love, that we walk after his commandments" (2 John 6). This is not to equate the commandments of Jesus with all the Mosaic Law. But it is quite clear that the biblical authors see no conflict between love and law as principles.

Far from being set against one another, law and love are inextricably connected. Love fulfills the law and the law is summed up in love. This chapter will consider how that relationship works and what it means for the Christian who seeks to love others.

"Do Unto Others"

Near the end of his Sermon on the Mount, Jesus sums up the Old Testament commands for personal ethics with these words, "Therefore all things whatsoever ye would that men should do to you, do ye even so to them: for this is the law and the prophets" (Matt 7:12). This command, often called the Golden Rule and expressed with the simpler language, "Do unto others as you would have them do unto you," articulates the Old Testament command to "Love your neighbor as yourself." While, as we said before, Jesus presents the Christian obligation to love one another as Christ has loved us as a new command with a higher standard, it is helpful to consider this Golden Rule and to build up from it.

This rule is profound in its simplicity and its easy application is virtually every aspect of life. It is, I would say, the basis for most of our notions of "common courtesy." The basic way we treat everyone we encounter should reflect how we would prefer to be treated. When driving, I would that men not cut me off and that, when I cut them off, they not take it as a personal attack or a sign that I am utterly incompetent. So, when driving, I try not to cut others off and, when I am cut off, I try not to think poorly of the driver who did it. When I ask someone a question, I like to be answered. So, when someone contacts me personally with a question, I try to answer that person. Opening doors, including people in conversation, wiping our feet before entering a home, and many other simple courteous actions reflect not so much specific training in etiquette as fulfillment of the Golden Rule.

What is interesting about the Golden Rule, when fully considered, is that it leads to an inversion of standards. The standard I would apply to others I instead apply to myself, while the standard I would apply to myself I instead apply to others. We should be honest; most of us have a double standard where our selves are concerned. Have you ever been listening to an anecdote, and you can tell the person telling the story expects you to be on his side, but the facts of the story as you hear it put that person squarely in the wrong? Or, maybe it just seems to you like a situation where there is blame to go around. But the person telling the story, quite naturally and unconsciously, sees things differently. The deck is tilted slightly in his favor. But the command to love means we must consciously tilt the deck the other way. Do you want people to hear your stories and presume you are probably in the right? Then you are obligated to presume the others are probably in the right. Loving one another means exchanging places with all other people in the way in which we think about each other.

Do you want others to tell you the truth? Then you must tell them the truth. Do you want others to meet a high standard? Then you must meet a high standard. Do you want others to arrive on time? Then you must arrive on time. Do you want others to apologize and ask for your forgiveness when they wrong you? Then you must apologize and ask for forgiveness when you wrong others. And, you must do all this unilaterally; you do not treat them this way so that they will treat you the same way. You treat them this way because your Lord has commanded it.

Conversely, do you want others to trust you? Then you must be trusting. Do you want others to understand that sometimes you cannot do your absolute best? Then you must understand that about others. Do you want others to presume the best about you when you miss an appointment, make a mistake, or lose your temper? Then you must presume the best about them when they do these things. Do you want others to occasionally overlook your sins without you having to clearly and specifically apologize for them? Then you must be willing to do the same. And, again, this is all unilateral. This is you thinking through the way you would tilt the world in your favor, if you could, and choosing to willfully flip it over so that you grant to others all the benefits you would reserve for yourself.

I recognize that, as you look through this list of questions, your answer to some of them may be, "No." Maybe you do not want other people to trust you. Maybe you do not want others to meet a high standard of quality in the work that they perform for you. Maybe it is okay with you if others are late or if they never speak with you again if you offend them in the slightest. We are all different, and the reality is that we do not all have the same expectations of how we would be treated or how we would treat others. The good thing is that, since we invert to whom our standards apply, minor differences in this regard make little difference.

I like traditional manners in most situations. I do not know how important they are, exactly, but I believe our nation was in a better place when people followed them than it is since they fell out of favor. So, when I was a Ph.D. candidate, I never entered my major professor's office without being invited. I was like a vampire; I would loom outside his door until he invited me in. I also never sat down without being invited or without first asking, "Mind if I have a seat?" He never mentioned it, so I have no idea if he noticed this, cared about it, appreciated it, or thought it strange. It was my effort to be polite and thereby show respect and appreciation for his time and effort. Since then, when I have had students come to my office, I am always quick to verbally invite them in and offer them a seat. I usually stand as they enter, and always do if they are ladies. Since my goal now is to be welcoming and available for my part, my students do not need to share my eccentric attachment to older manners. They are my standards for myself, not for them. We can differ about many such matters and, as long as our focus is on loving rather than being loved, there will not be problems.

"Make Us God"

However, while we can differ on how we would like to be treated in some ways without it causing problems, the potential for larger differences in how individuals desire to be treated show that the command, "Love your neighbor as yourself," is in a sense incomplete. Consider a young male who is attempting to pressure his date into fornication. His argument goes like this. I would like for you to have sex with me, so I should have sex with you. You would like for me to respect your position on sexual purity, so you should respect my position, which is that it is less important than our enjoyment. So, you should have sex with me. If the Golden Rule is all this young lady has to go by, this is a fairly solid argument from love to fornication, at least if she wants to be convinced.

What is missing from this argument? Quite simply, a rule is missing. In this case, the rule that is missing is, "This is the desire of God, your sanctification, that you should abstain from fornication" (1 Thess 4:3). God's desire is that this young lady abstain from fornication. God's desire is also that she should love. So, either God is incoherent or abstaining from fornication is loving, all arguments aside.

God has given us laws so that, in many common circumstances, we know what is loving, all arguments aside. When considering matters such as adultery, murder, or fornication, we do not need to consider whether John would want Jill to commit one of them and whether that would make it okay for him to do so. Not all "things whatsoever ye would that men should do to you" deserve equal consideration. On some of these matters, God has spoken. When God has spoken, our responsibility is to conform what we desire others to do to us to His standard. Our standards in some matters are not reliable enough to ground proper love.

We are accustomed to thinking of Old Testament Israel as a people burdened with a complex set of laws from God. It is important to recognize that is not how they started. They started as people called into a simple, personal, covenant relationship with God. In Exodus 19 God offers them, "Now therefore, if ye will obey my voice indeed, and keep my covenant, then ye shall be a peculiar treasure unto me above all people: for all the earth *is* mine And ye shall be unto me a kingdom of priests, and an holy nation" (vv. 5-6). Yet, after promising to obey God, they violate His first call to them. He told them, after three days, when they heard the trumpet, they were to go up into the mount (v. 13). Yet when the trumpet sounds louder and louder, the people refuse to go (v. 19). God speaks to Israel the Ten Commandments, but the people will not hear any more from God and send Moses in their place. After this, the people are not allowed to come up any more (cf. Exod 24:2). Then, they violate the command, which they had heard from God Himself, to make no graven image. They say to Aaron, "make us God," that is, a graven image, for them to worship (Exodus 32). After this, they receive more laws, now about the tabernacle and the priestly office. Then, Nadab and Abihu, priests, sin and violate the rules regarding offering incense (Leviticus 10). Israel receives more laws. This cycle continues, with Israel sinning and, as a result, receiving more laws. As Paul says, the law "was added because of transgressions" (Gal 3:19). Because the people kept violating the simple laws they had, God gave them more detailed, more specific, more restrictive laws.

There are several purposes for these Old Testament laws, most of which are not relevant to this discussion. But what is relevant is that God, even in His dealing with ancient Israel, is not first and foremost concerned with giving them laws. He gives them laws because they show themselves unable to do what they should without them.[4] Israel breaks the law to make no graven images. So, God provides more extensive laws for how they can worship Him properly, all without graven images. But Abraham, who apparently did worship God properly (cf. Gen 25:6), never needed and thus never received such extensive laws.

The specific laws of God, whether those he gives to Israel or those He gives to the church, are a "how-to manual" for carrying out the basic expectations God has for man. Consider, for example, Micah 6:8, "He hath shewed thee, O man, what

---

[4] And unable to do what they should with them as well. There is no doubt one of the purposes of the Mosaic Law is to show that law alone can never change man's heart.

is good; and what doth the LORD require of thee, but to do justly, and to love mercy, and to walk humbly with thy God?" Micah is not saying that an Israelite should ignore the Mosaic Law and just do these three things. He is saying that following the Mosaic Law is grounded in these. Not holding the man who kills a thief breaking in guilty of murder is an example of what it means "to do justly." Releasing slaves during the Sabbath Year and the Jubilee were concrete manifestations of what it meant to "love mercy." Bringing one's proper offerings before God were specific ways one might "walk humbly" with God. This is how Jesus can say the Pharisees, who tithed mint and cummin, should have also attended the "weightier *matters* of the law, judgment, mercy, and faith" (Matt 23:23). Some matters are weightier. Indeed, there are clear parallels here between "doing justly" and "judgment," "loving mercy" and "mercy," and "walking humbly" and "faith." They are core principles which are then articulated for Israel, in particular, in the rest of the Mosaic Law. And Jesus connects these particulars, all the law and the prophets, to the command to love.

"An Eye for an Eye"

In Exodus 21, God lays out His law for responding to harm to a pregnant woman that also harms the child with the painful litany, "Life for life, eye for eye, tooth for tooth, hand for hand, foot for foot, burning for burning, wound for wound, stripe for stripe" (v. 23-25). Similar expressions are seen in Lev 24:20 and Deut 19:21. This expression of retributive justice, sometimes referred to with the Latin *lex talionis*, is often used to characterize the Mosaic Law as harsh and unloving, the very opposite of the Christian position. Even Jesus seemed to find fault with it in the Sermon on the Mount (Matt 5:38-39).

However, this understanding of *lex talionis* is mistaken. First, it ignores that within the Mosaic Law itself it is made clear that the full extent of these words need not always be applied. Immediately following these words we see that a master who knocks the tooth out of his servant does not lose a tooth, but instead loses that servant (Exod 21:27). A man whose ox, known to be unruly and dangerous, kills another may be allowed to ransom his life depending upon the choice of the victim's family and the judges (Exod 21:30-31, cf. v. 22). Thus, *lex talionis* represents a limit upon retaliation under the law. You can take no more than an eye for an eye, no more than a life for a life. It prohibits escalation, not mercy. Second, understanding *lex talionis* to be harsh ignores the true harshness seen in many law codes from similar times. For example, the death penalty is commanded in the Code of Hammurabi (1700s B.C.) for buying from a representative without witnesses or a contract, not being able to pay fines for theft, selling stolen goods, and potentially simply for stealing. The Mosaic Law never sanctions capital punishment for property crimes.[5] Third, this understanding of *lex talionis* ignores that the Mosaic Law is a combination of personal and societal obligations. It is this confusion which Jesus has in

---

[5] It does defend a man who kills an intruding thief in the act, but that is a very different thing (Exod 22:2).

mind in the Sermon on the Mount. "An eye for an eye" does not mean that I, personally, must respond to all actions against me with commensurate retribution. I can turn the other cheek and leave such matters to God. Society with its appropriate authorities does have a responsibility of executing justice, as Romans 13 confirms in the New Testament, but that is distinct from a personal response of wrath or hatred for those who wrong me.

"Keep My Commandments"

What does this mean for us? It means that the specific commands of the Bible model what it means to love. The commands regarding how we are to treat God model what it means to love God. As Jesus said, "If ye love me, keep my commandments" (John 14:15). The commands regarding how we treat each other model what it means to love each other.

Model is an important word here. Christians are not bound by the Mosaic Law, as law. Its status as law has been fulfilled by Christ (Matt 5:17-18, Rom 10:4). But the Mosaic Law articulated specific guidance for living a life of love for God's people, Israel, at a certain time and place. We can see in all those commands things that matter to God and should therefore matter to us. Similarly, New Testament commands articulate God's specific instruction to His people, the church, on how they should love one another. It is easy to note how much more general and less specific many of these commands are. Indeed, many times we find not so much commands as descriptions of the character and behavior presumed to be present within a church of God's redeemed saints. And this means that, as long as we are the church, it is in the way God has instructed the church that we are to carry out His command to love one another.

This means that we are not free to disobey some New Testament commands or disregard New Testament principles in developing our understanding and implementation of love. We cannot claim to be more loving than Jesus or to better understand love than Paul or John. Beyond the basic guidance of the Golden Rule we have clear, normative, authoritative instructions on how to love one another. These next chapters will try to bring some of these to bear on the challenge of deciding how to love one another.

Reflection Questions

1. As you think about the laws, the rules, in Scripture, does any one stand out as seeming particularly loving to you? Why do you think that is?

2. Does any law or rule stand out as particularly unloving or contrary to love to you? Why do you think that is?

3. Have you ever consciously decided to break one of God's laws thinking that was loving? Did that bring about the highest good for the people involved? What highest good was that?

"No Respect of Persons"

We live in a world of celebrities. There have certainly been famous people in the past, but at no prior point in history has a culture had 24/7 video, audio, and print access to the lives of others. Jesus was famous in his day. Throngs of people followed him. People wondered where he was and what he was doing. But of the details of his life we have little more than the four Gospels as record, 135 pages in the Bible in my hand. I dare say more words have been written about Brad and Angelina or Kate's new baby or whatever celebrity of our day in *People* or the *National Inquirer* than were written about Jesus in his day. And, the interest in celebrities often affects more people than one might think. I remember being shocked when, as a pastor of an aging rural church, I found out that one of my older ladies, around ninety years old, was deeply interested in and knew everything about Anna Nicole Smith's baby.

In a world of celebrities, we are accustomed to them being treated differently than "the common folk." I remember hearing a news report about Tom Cruise's security detail clearing out a restroom at some event so that their principal could have special privacy. Celebrities sometimes appear to "get off easy" in court, even when convicted of criminal actions. Politicians, often celebrities in their own right as they practice what has been called "showbiz for the ugly," engage in boorish and sometimes criminal behavior without consequence. Even on a small scale, celebrity affects how people are treated. My high school had a football team that was consistently state- and nationally-ranked. Their buses often received police escort, complete with flashing lights and sirens at the ready, to away games. That never happened for the debate team bus.

God does not exactly address celebrity in the Bible. But, He does clearly address treating different people differently; that is, according to different standards. His rule is simple: Do not do it. He is not a respecter of persons, and Christians should not be either.

That God is no respecter of persons is a direct statement of Scripture that is made several times. Peter says, after seeing that God provided salvation through Christ unto the Gentile, Cornelius, "Of a truth I perceive that God is no respecter of persons" (Acts 10:34). In 2 Chronicles 19, Jehoshaphat places respect of persons in parallel with iniquity, with sin, and denies that either is found in God. Paul, in the process of showing both Jew and Gentile to be equally under the judgment of God, notes, "There is no respect of persons with God" (Rom 2:11).

Because God is no respecter of persons, He charges His people to be the same. These charges are often connected with the obligation to deliver righteous judgment (e.g., Lev 19:15, Deut 1:17, 16:19, Prov 24:23). In James 2, however, this charge is presented more generally, as a prohibition against generally treating some classes of persons differently than others. When one considers other ways in which the New Testament breaks down barriers among different classes of persons, it is clear that this command is relevant for all Christians, not just judges.

On the other hand, at times God is specifically said to respect individual persons as opposed to others. God "had respect unto Abel . . . but unto Cain . . . He had not respect" (Gen 4:4-5). "God looked upon the children of Israel," a group of persons, "and God had respect unto them" (Exod 2:25). God promises to the Israelites who keep his commandments, "I will have respect unto you, and make you fruitful, and multiply you, and establish my covenant with you" (Lev 26:9). So, the assertion that God does not respect persons and the corollary command that believers not respect persons need some interpretation.

"Worse than an Infidel"

The care of widows was an important issue in the early church. There was not the vast "safety net" of government social programs that there is in America today. Community, and usually religious, organizations met the needs of the old and infirm. In Acts 6, the church deals with an issue of provision for widows by appointing the first deacons to wait tables. Paul, in his instructions to the younger pastor Timothy, lays out some more specific guidelines for how the church should care for widows. While he acknowledges the basic responsibility of the church to care for its widows, he writes, "But if any provide not for his own, and specially for those of his own house, he hath denied the faith, and is worse than an infidel" (1 Tim 5:8). Indeed, three times in this paragraph, he returns to this point (5:4, 8, 16); family members have a higher obligation to care for their widows than the church as a whole.

This is one example that shows that the command to love one another, and not respect persons while doing so, is not a command to treat all others, or even all other believers, the same. If a man in the church has a widowed mother and knows another needy person in the next pew, he is not equally obligated to take care of each. If he has $100, Paul's words cannot properly be read to mean that he should give $50 to each. It is his responsibility to care for his mother; if he does not, he is "worse than an infidel."

It is better to think of the command to not show partiality as a command to treat people in a specific relationship to one according to the same set of rules. It does not mean we must treat our children like our employers. But it does mean that we must treat all our children according to the same standards. That Jacob treated his children with partiality, loving Joseph more than his brothers, is presented as a clear negative, with negative consequences (Gen 37:3-4). The Mosaic Law forbade a man who had a servant wife from treating her worse than any other wife (Exod 21:10). We do not treat spouses like neighbors, but we should treat each of our neighbors according to the same standards.

"Submitting to One Another"

The command not to respect persons also cannot be read as a command to do away with all categories into which we group persons. In Ephesians 5, after discussing the glorious unity of the church of God, Paul transitions to some of the specific responsibilities believers have to one another with the language, "Submitting to one another in the fear of God" (Eph 5:21). While this language is sometimes taken out of context to present some sort of generic leveling of people within the church, its proper meaning, as shown in the commands that follow, is that specific persons in the church have specific responsibilities towards other persons within the church. Wives submit to husbands while husbands love wives. Children obey parents while fathers raise them properly. Servants obey and faithfully serve masters while masters treat their servants honorably, remembering that God does not respect persons (Eph 6:9).

These are not the only categories into which people are divided in the New Testament. There are pastors, elders, overseers, and the flock; old and young men and women; single, divorced, and unmarried persons; masters and slaves; husbands and wives; children and parents; authorities; and more. The New Testament does not suggest that we do away with all such categories. Instead, it charges the members of each to behave properly and lovingly where they are in executing the responsibilities they have. As Paul says, "let every man, wherein he is called, therein abide with God" (1 Cor 7:24). These categories are not things Christians need to strive to overturn.

"A Gift Blinds the Eyes of the Wise"

What, then, does the command to not respect persons mean? As noted before, the primary context of the command is that of judgment. In that context, two concerns arise. The first is expressed in Deut 16:19, "Thou shalt not wrest judgment; thou shalt not respect persons, neither take a gift." We should not treat people differently according to what we can gain from them.

This is, when considered this way, very consistent with the command to love one another. Loving is about giving, not gaining. Yet it is very tempting to treat those from whom we hope to gain something better than those from whom we want nothing, particularly in seemingly minor details. When you are listening to your phone messages or looking through your e-mails, whom do you answer first? Is it the person from whom you hope to get something? When you see the name or hear the voice of that person who is always asking for something, do you move on? Is that the person to whom you will get back to later . . . maybe? Treating those in a position to do something for you better than those who are not is not the sort of love Christ commands.

Jesus said as much himself. He was invited one Sabbath to the house of a Pharisee to dine. While there, he said to his host:

> When you make a morning or evening meal, do not call your friends or your brothers or your relatives or your rich neighbors. They might invite you in turn and repay you. No, whenever you have a party, call the poor, the maimed, the lame, and the blind. And you will be blessed; because they do not have repayment for you, it will be repaid to you in the resurrection of the righteous (Luke 14:12-14).

Note that it is not even the desire to get something back that Jesus cautions against. It is the possibility that one might be repaid that is the negative. The people invited are either in a position to help the host out, or they are not.

It would be a mistake to make this command an absolute. Jesus is a guest at the wedding in Cana of Galilee without making such demands. Never inviting one's brothers to a meal goes against the biblical appreciation for family. But the gist of the command is clear. Our love for others should not take into consideration whether they are in a position to reward us. It is the Father who will do that at the resurrection. James says just giving the well-dressed man a better seat than the poorly dressed man is sin (James 2:2-4, 9).

"Thou Shalt not Respect the Person of the Poor"

At the same time, the Bible warns against inappropriately favoring those in need. Lev 19:15 reads, "Ye shall do no unrighteousness in judgment: thou shalt not respect the person of the poor, nor honour the person of the mighty: but in righteousness shalt thou judge thy neighbor." This does not appear to have been much of a temptation in Jesus' time. The New Testament does not echo this side of the command. Instead, it presents the religious people of the day as disdainful of and willing to oppress the poor. James says to his audience, "Ye have despised the poor" (James 2:6). In Mark 12:40-42, Jesus rebukes the Pharisees for devouring the houses of widows and then commends the poor widow for giving freely of the little she has.

Today, however, there is often a tendency to favor those who are in need, or are perceived to be in need, in some way. People defend those who illegally cross the borders of the

United States by pointing out that they are poor people from poor countries, so their crimes should be overlooked. An American jury found for almost three million dollars in punitive damages against McDonald's when a customer spilled hot coffee on herself. How can one explain such a decision, except by noting that the corporation is rich and the individual is comparatively poor? In America, some minority students are given preferential treatment in college admissions not for anything that they have done individually, but because of past injustices that have put many of them, without a doubt, in difficult situations.

It is important to note that what is being discussed is not generosity or alms for those in need; that is specifically commanded by Scripture. But to wrest justice from others to treat the poor better is unjust. And, it is unjust even if the poor and the other are not in direct conflict with each other. Consider, for example, an employer who has two part-time employees, one of whom is needy while the other has recently won the lottery. The needy one is not a particularly good worker. He arrives late, takes days off unexpectedly, and is not always productive when he is at work. The lottery winner is a model employee. One day, a full-time position becomes open. Whom should the employer, if he is a Christian charged to love, promote?

One might be tempted to say the needy one. The new position will provide him with more income, which his family could use. And, after all, the other guy is rich; hiring the poor man full-time does not harm him. Or, does it? Is there more to a job, a promotion, recognition of work well done, than money? And, what of the other employees? Do they benefit, or are they harmed, when a subpar worker is promoted simply because he is poor? What about customers? Should they receive worse or less consistent service more often? In so many decisions to show partiality, others are affected as a side effect.

"Judges According to Every Man's Work"

Of course, there are many other grounds upon which people show partiality. People have shown partiality according to race in many cultures across many centuries. People show partiality to family beyond the basic familial closeness the Bible presumes; they wrest judgment to favor their family. People are partial to friends as well.

After its founding, many positions in the executive branch of the federal government were awarded according to what was called "the spoils system." When a new President came to power, he replaced, at will, those in executive positions with people of his own. In time, this system was abused enough that the citizens demanded reform, which came first in the form of the Pendleton Act of 1881. Now, most executives in the federal government do not need to fear for their jobs just because a new President is elected.

Unfortunately, while the spoils system has been mostly rooted out of the federal executive, it is rampant in Christendom. I have personally seen it in churches and other Christian organizations. A new leader is hired for a position and suddenly his wife, cousin, friends, and previous employees have positions as well. Those who held the positions before are demoted or even dismissed. Upon witnessing the nepotism of one such leader, a librarian at a Christian institution remarked, "I am just lucky he did not have a brother-in-law who was a librarian." This sort of partiality is the farthest thing from loving one another.

As was noted earlier, God is said to be no respecter of persons. In the New Testament, this is twice mentioned in connection with God's method of judgment which is "according to every man's work" (1 Peter 1:17). Paul makes the point at greater length in Colossians, "And whatsoever ye do, do *it* heartily, as to the Lord, and not unto men; Knowing that of the Lord ye shall receive the reward of the inheritance: for ye serve the Lord Christ. But he that doeth wrong shall receive for the wrong which he hath done: and there is no respect of persons" (Col 3:23-25). How does God avoid respecting persons? He does so by rewarding men according to their works.

This is, then, part of God's recipe for loving one another. We do not show partiality, but instead treat people as their conduct merits. If a rich man commits murder, he should be convicted of murder and sentenced accordingly. If a poor person commits murder, he should be convicted of murder and sentenced accordingly. God through Moses warns against showing partiality because of pity (Deut 19:13). Nor should other factors be involved; race, sex, or even kinship with the judge are all irrelevant. People who bear us similar relationships who engage in similar behavior should be treated similarly.

Many perceive this idea, of treating people according to

their works, as going against a grain in our shared Christian faith. That grain is grace. Grace, God's unmerited favor towards man, is the basis for his saving relationship with Christians. "By grace are ye saved," Paul writes (Eph 2:8). If God has favor on a man who does not deserve it, and Christians are to imitate God, then should they not show favor to others who do not deserve it? God saves the sinner who does not deserve it. Should I not promote the slack worker who does not deserve it?

Not exactly, for a couple of reasons. The first is that "unmerited" does not mean "unreasoned." God's grace for sinners is unmerited, undeserved. But it is not bestowed in a random or reasonless fashion. God is gracious to those who trust in Him, who believe on Him. As a parallel, consider the tooth fairy. Now, for a child to receive money, or anything else, simply because he has lost a tooth is unmerited. Losing a tooth does not deserve payment. But when a child receives money from the tooth fairy, it is not a reasonless or random event. She has lost a tooth, and then receives the money. If the tooth fairy starts giving out money after every haircut, then something is wrong. Similarly, God grants righteousness and forgiveness to those who trust in Him (e.g., Gen 15:6). This is not merited; I owe God my trust already. I deserve no special reward for giving it to Him. But it is not unreasoned. There is a connection between righteousness and faith that God has put in place. This reason also results in consistency.

So, the believer who follows God should be lovingly gracious, but that graciousness should be reasoned and consistent. Consider, for example, Joe, who goes out with a couple of friends, Bill and Scott. While at dinner the trio get into an argument, with Bill and Scott on one side and Joe on the other. The argument elevates in the parking lot into violence, with Bill and Scott joining together to give Joe a brief but painful drubbing before they part ways. How should Joe respond to this? On the one hand, Joe is commanded to, while he stands praying, forgive those against whom he has anything (Mark 11:25). In some sense he lets go of the animosity and resentment he might feel towards both men. This is certainly gracious. But there is another sense of forgiveness which Jesus says can be contingent upon repentance (Luke 17:4), the forgiveness we might call restoration. The next day, Bill comes to Joe, clearly ashamed and saddened at his poor behavior the night before. He expresses his sorrow and regret and commits to not treating Joe this way again. Joe sees Scott later that day, and Scott laughs at the memory of mistreating Joe. Is it biblical for Joe to treat Scott and Bill the same at this point? Is it loving? Not at all. Until Scott acknowledges his wrong, there is something between the men which Joe cannot properly pretend is not there. Thus Joe is gracious to both men, and not partial. But the way his grace applies to the two men differs according to their behavior.

The second reason love and grace do not mean the undeserving worker should be promoted over the deserving is because of an aspect of love mentioned earlier. Love means acting at expense to one's self to bring about the good of others. It does not mean acting at expense to others. The amazing thing about God's saving grace is that the Triune God alone bears the burden of it. It was the Father who poured out His wrath upon His only-begotten Son, forsaking Him to the judgment deserved by sinful humanity. It was the Son who drank the cup of God's wrath to the bitterest dregs. He died, the just for the unjust. God alone paid the price for the grace He extends to sinners.

This is why love does not countenance partiality in judgment. When one is deciding between Jill and Jane, giving Jill better than she deserves almost certainly means giving Jane worse than she deserves. Partiality means doing good for another not at expense to self, but at expense to others. That is not love.

It should also be noted that the one who abandons partiality in judgment shows a willingness to make two types of sacrifices. If one could not benefit from partiality in judgment, God would not have to warn us against it. There are external and internal rewards to being partial which one gives up when he judges impartially.

As a young man, a couple of my friends and I worked at an institution that was, among other things, a halfway house for paroled federal prisoners. One of our inmates, whom we will call Murphy, was a bank robber whose loot had never been recovered. So, from time to time he would return from the sort of low-level work someone recently paroled could get with a $1000 leather jacket. It was eventually discovered that he was bribing the weekend night clerk to let him go out at night. One of my friends asked Murphy why he had never offered such a bribe to one of us. He said, "I knew you guys wouldn't go for it." The person known to judge without bribes should not expect to get one.

When we are known to judge justly, we give up all the potential bribes others might offer us. These are not necessarily monetary, of course. We give up the potential "friends" who might befriend us in hopes of influencing our judgments. We give up the potential favors we might be offered in hopes of receiving favors in return. These sacrifices of potential external rewards show a willingness to sacrifice for the good of others.

We also, by judging according to what has been done, give up a powerful internal reward, personal power. Imagine the employer above who promotes the poor worker over the good one. On what basis has he done so? Simply because he could. He can view his decision as an act of personal magnanimity. He can think of himself as kind and thoughtful and powerful all at the same time. Most of us can think of someone we know, or perhaps just a government worker we encounter, who seems to relish the ability to make arbitrary decisions regarding others. These decisions can seem minor or petty to us, but seem immensely important to the one making them. But when we are impartial in judgment, we give up that sense of power. The decisions we make do not rest upon our personal dispositions, but upon what God has deemed just. We humble ourselves in these decisions. We love.

"Atop All these, Love"

In Col 3:12-14, Paul beseeches the church to deal lovingly with one another, forbearing and forgiving. As we close out our consideration of the command to avoid partiality, it is useful to consider applying this in the church. One thing which should be emphasized is that our impartiality should result in us treating all our fellow believers as we would treat those we like best. It is easy to forgive some people, the ones we like, and hold grudges against others, the ones we do not. It is easy to give those we like the benefit of the doubt, and withhold it from those we do not like. We might be more generous with those we like, more tolerant, and more patient. All of these are temptations to resist.

It is natural that we will like some people more than others. We will have more in common with them, find them more interesting, share common experiences or frames of reference, and so on. But the command to love one another must not be sabotaged by our liking some more than others. Maybe your church has multiple elders, and you like some more than others. That affection may affect with whom you watch the ball game, but it should never affect how you treat them in matters beyond those friendly activities. You may not like that guy who sits in the second row, but that should not prevent you from taking his family a meal in their grief, helping him out with bills in his need, or pitching in to help him move a couch. Christ's command is to love one another, without partiality. So, the next time you are "offended" by or take exception to someone you do not like, ask yourself if it would bother you if your close friend did the same thing. Unless someone does something that genuinely merits a different type of treatment, we have a responsibility to treat people similarly. Deciding when different treatment is merited is something we will consider next.

Reflection Questions

1. Whom are you most likely to treat with favoritism? Why?

2. Whom are you least likely to treat with favoritism?

3. What would things be like if you treated the person you named for 2. like the person you named for 1?

"I Will Go Down Now, and See"

In Genesis 19, God destroys Sodom and Gomorrah for the grievous sins they have committed. He is their Creator (Isa 40:28), Possessor (Gen 14:22), and Judge (Gen 18:25), and so it is His responsibility to do so. As the one who knows the actions, words, and even thoughts of men (Psalm 139:1-4), He is competent to judge perfectly.

One of the interesting things about the story in Genesis 19, however, is that in it God does not judge simply on the basis of His perfect knowledge. Instead, He acts as an investigator or detective. He says to Abraham, "Because the cry of Sodom and Gomorrah is great, and because their sin is very grievous. I will go down now, and see whether they have done altogether according to the cry of it, which is come unto me; and if not, I will know" (Gen 18:20-21). He speaks as if He has heard a report of a crime and must now investigate it. He does not go by what He has heard or what He simply knows, as the omniscient God that He is. He "goes down" to see. This "going down" takes the form of two of the "men" going to Sodom and encountering and then rescuing Lot in Sodom. Sailhamer suggests that "the third man went to Gomorrah and investigated that city."[6] God goes down to the cities of the plain before destroying them in judgment.

---

[6]John Sailhamer, *The Pentateuch as Narrative: A Biblical-Theological Commentary* (Grand Rapids: Zondervan, 1992), 169.

Why would God do this? The biblical picture of God is of a God who has perfect knowledge (Job 37:16). He does not need to "go down" to know what is transpiring on earth; He "looks down" from heaven (e.g., Psalm 14:2). The answer is that this is a lesson to Abraham and to us, the readers. He has just introduced a new concept of Abraham's role in the world, that of teaching his children to do righteousness and justice (Gen 18:19). So He, in turn, wants to show Abraham how it is done. A just judge goes down to see. He does not go by the cry that reaches his ears. He does not operate on rumors or possibility. He goes down to see.

This responsibility, for judges to fully investigate matters, is similarly presented in the Mosaic Law. When men have a controversy, they stand before the Lord, priests, and judges and the last "make diligent inquisition" into the matter (Deut 19:18). If a man's goods are lost in the care of another, and the man who had care of them says a thief did it, the judges are to investigate the matter (Exod 22:8). When a body is found between cities, the "elders and . . . judges shall come forth" (Deut 21:2) to determine which city has jurisdiction in the matter. Judging justly is a serious responsibility in Scripture.

But Jesus forbade judgment, did he not? A verse every naughty church-goer, along with many of the less naughty, is quick to learn is Matt 7:1, "Judge not, lest ye be judged." But this sweeping statement cannot be properly understood as a prohibition of judgment. Instead, the next verse clarifies that this is, in fact, the Golden Rule again. Jesus continues, "For with what judgment ye judge, ye shall be judged: and with what measure ye mete, it shall be measured to you again"

(Matt 7:2). That is, the way that you judge others will play a role in how you are judged. The way you measure out rewards or condemnation to others will play a role in how these are measured out to you. So, judge as you would like to be judged. But no believer can escape all forms of judgment; "We shall all stand before the judgment seat of Christ" (Rom 14:10). If no believer can escape all forms of judgment, it follows that Jesus is not here forbidding all forms of judgment. He is forbidding harsh condemnation before which we ourselves could not stand.

Now, you may be thinking, What does this have to do with me? I am no judge. But we all are judges. We constantly make decisions about other people. We make decisions at work, at home, at school, and at church. We judge where to buy staples and where to get dinner. We judge those we associate with and those who associate with our children. When we hear that the pastor's car was seen in a certain unsavory place at a certain unsavory time, we make a judgment. And there is nothing wrong with this, by the way. Paul looks to the church to contain people competent to make judgments. He rebukes the Corinthians for taking each other to court, reminding them that the saints will judge the world; there certainly should be some among them who can judge within the church (1 Cor 6:1-5). The question for us is not whether we should judge. The question is how to judge lovingly.

"I Will Know It"

The first point of loving judgment is that already mentioned, that it is based upon knowledge and investigation, not rumor or hearsay. Just the other night my wife and I watched a movie called *Survivor*. In it, a security specialist in the London visa office narrowly escapes a bombing, flees for safety and, as a result, is deemed a suspect who must be brought in dead or alive. As I was watching it, I realized how many movie plots would simply unravel if this basic commandment, that of investigating before judging, were followed.

In American law, we are supposed to be innocent until proven guilty. We can argue about whether this is really how things work before the law, but I do not doubt that many of us can point to instances in which just an accusation, just a suggestion of impropriety, has harmed a believer because others judged before any investigation was done into the matter. John's car was seen where? Well, he was up to no good.

While I was in college, myself and several friends worked for the same company, an island of believers in a small mission field. At one point, one of the young women with whom we worked, call her Tessa, had car trouble and wanted a lift home. One of my friends, call him Shawn, got off work when she did and was an ideal candidate to give her a lift. But he would not. He would not because he was engaged, and he was concerned that someone he knew might see him alone in his car with Tessa, an attractive woman about his age. Shawn was confident that this would result in rumors that would be a problem, and I cannot say that he was wrong.

Note the chain reaction of anti-love this willingness to judge without knowledge caused. If your car was in the shop, would you not like for an other to give you a ride home? Of course you would. So, loving his neighbor as himself should have led Shawn to give Tessa a ride home. If you were seen with someone other than your significant other, would you want people to trust your fidelity or at least ask you about it before they started gossiping? Of course you would. Even the most basic application of the Golden Rule would mean not saying anything about Shawn until the facts were known. But here what I would consider basic courtesy, not even something as demanding as Christian love, was almost thwarted by a loveless approach to judgment.[7] How many potentially loving deeds have been thwarted or colored with fear because of unjust judgment? How many men have failed to minister to women, or vice versa, because of the assumptions that follow the rampant immorality in our society? In order to love, we must investigate matters before we judge.

So, what form should this investigation take? Going back to the basic rule of love, you should investigate the way you would want to be investigated before judgment is passed. But beyond this, God has given several clear guidelines.

The first is that accusations should be supported by eyewitnesses, multiple witnesses of the same event who can

---

[7] Tessa did get a ride home from a Christian, but it was not Shawn.

independently corroborate one another's testimony. In the Mosaic Law, multiple witnesses are required to condemn a person to death (Num 35:30, Deut 17:6), or indeed to testify against him "in any sin that he sinneth" (Deut 19:15). Jesus seems to confirm this expectation when he discusses sin amongst the brethren in Matthew 18, saying, "But if he will not hear thee, then take with thee one or two more, that in the mouth of two or three witnesses every word may be established" (v. 16). Jesus even appeals to multiple witnesses other than himself to confirm who he is and what he is doing in John 5. He says the people could listen to John the Baptist, but his better witnesses are the works which he does (v. 36) and God the Father (v. 37). Paul instructs Timothy to not receive an accusation against an elder without multiple witnesses (1 Tim 5:19). And, these witnesses must agree substantially about what they witness; the Sanhedrin, corrupt as it was, could not convict Christ on the testimony of the false witnesses because they did not agree (Mark 14:56, 59). Certainly, loving judgement requires evidence at least as good as that required by the court that judicially murdered Jesus.

The second is that the person accused should be confronted as discreetly as possible before anything else happens. Again, how would you like to be treated if someone heard or saw something troubling about you? Would you like him to spread it all about town? Would you like him to judge you without hearing from you at all? Of course not. And so Jesus commands believers who have been sinned against to go privately to the culprit (Matt 18:15). How much more should one who has simply fallen under suspicion be given an opportunity to speak before he is judged.

Finally, inconclusive investigations are to be left to God, not judged as if they were conclusive. In Numbers 5, God presents how to deal with a situation when a man suspects his wife of infidelity but there is no witness or other evidence against her. The couple brings an offering before the Lord and the priest calls upon God to judge the matter. Deuteronomy 21 describes a similar situation in which an offering is made by the elders of a city who cannot determine who killed a person within its jurisdiction. They leave the matter to God.

This is very difficult, especially considering many of the matters which call for judgement today. When the only people involved in a situation are, say, a young man and a young woman, it can be tempting to assume the worst, despite whatever protestations they make. But this is exactly the sort of thing God says must be left to Him, if the two are willing to avow their innocence before Him. In many ways, it is easier to "make a decision and stick with it" and decide the person is either innocent or guilty than it is to leave the matter open to God. But this is part of God's instruction, and thus part of what it means to truly love one another.

It is worth repeating that "judge," throughout this discussion, does not necessarily have a legal meaning or carry the idea of condemnation. We might substitute, "evaluate." How will you evaluate other believers? If a believer needs a job but you have heard "through the grapevine" that he is lazy, will you go by what you have heard or will you give him a shot and see if he is actually lazy? If you ask him about it and he acknowledges that he has been lazy in the past but wants to change, will you give him that opportunity? Will you risk cost to yourself to bring about that fellow believer's good? Remember; that is what it means to love.

"Fully Persuaded"

Throughout the fourth century, the Church faced a constant threat called Arianism. This belief system denied that Christ was fully God in the same sense that the Father was God. However, because it allowed that Jesus was the highest creature, a sort of lesser deity under the Father, it could be hard to detect. You could ask if Jesus was divine, deity, or even god, and the Arian could say, "Sure." But he was not really God, not the God of Abraham, Isaac, and Jacob.

To respond to the Arian crisis, the Church held the First Ecumenical Council at Nicaea. There, it used the word *homoousios* to identify the essence of the Son to be the same essence as that of the Father. Athanasius would later state that this strong word was necessary to serve as a sure test against an Arian. He might call Jesus god, but he would not call him *homoousios* with the Father. This was one of the early tests Christians felt compelled to develop to clearly distinguish between the orthodox and the heterodox, between true believers and deceivers or pretenders. It was necessary to contend for the core truth that Jesus, the Word made flesh, was not a creature, but the Creator (John 1:1-3, 14).

There are still core truths for which the believer must contend. But not everything I believe is such a truth. Many aspects of behavior and belief about which believers disagree are not matters which should cause division, are not matters which distinguish the faithful from the faithless. Paul discusses this issue at length in Romans 14. He begins:

> Him that is weak in the faith receive ye, but not to doubtful disputations. For one believeth that he may eat all things: another, who is weak, eateth herbs. Let not him that eateth despise him that eateth not; and let not him which eateth not judge him that eateth: for God hath received him. Who art thou that judgest another man's servant? to his own master he standeth or falleth. Yea, he shall be holden up: for God is able to make him stand. One man esteemeth one day above another: another esteemeth every day alike. Let every man be fully persuaded in his own mind (Rom 14:1-6).

Note here that Paul raises the language of judgment. He is writing about how believers view one another and warning two categories, both the strong and the weak, about viewing one another negatively.

The Roman world was as multicultural as any place one might see today, and that plurality of culture was evident in Rome. As people came to know the Lord, they were integrated into a single church body, the unity of which was grounded in the unity of the members in Christ (Eph 2:11-22). However, bringing together people of a variety of backgrounds raised some potential tensions in the church about what was appropriate behavior. One concern was over meats. This was not a question of vegetarianism. The issue was that many meats were slaughtered within the context of pagan sacrifice or were, after being slaughtered, ceremonially dedicated to idols. This meat would then be sold in the marketplace. Some, who perhaps had been involved in this sort of worship in the past, were unwilling to buy and thus eat any of this meat for fear that it had been involved in idolatry (cf. 1 Cor 10:25-30). They are "weak," according to Paul, in the sense that their consciences will not allow them to fully claim their liberty in Christ (yet). Paul also mentions disputes over days of worship. Some are attached to traditional days of worship, perhaps even the new moons and Sabbaths of Jewish worship (Isa 1:13). In these matters, the strong, those who fully claim their freedoms in Christ, are not to despise the weak. On the other hand the weak, those who have not yet, because of their sensitive consciences, realized those freedoms, are not to pass judgment on the strong.

It is important to recognize the concrete form these commands take. Paul's concern is not that the strong, by eating meat, will make someone who commands them not to eat meat offered to idols angry. He is not concerned about the bossy in the church. He is concerned about those whose consciences genuinely prevent them from eating meat offered to idols. He is concerned that, if they see the strong eating this meat, they may be prompted to eat this meat themselves before their consciences are comfortable with this action. He says, "Judge this . . . that no man put a stumblingblock or an occasion to fall in his brother's way" (Rom 14:13). He is concerned that the strong may provoke the weak to stumble in his own walk, not that the weak will be concerned about the strong's walk. He has already commanded that those who do not eat should not judge those who do. And, just to show we are not losing sight of love, Paul ends this discussion with the general command, "Let every one of us please his neighbor for his good to edification" (Rom 15:2), which is another way of stating the command to love. I please my neighbor for his good. I desire his good and act to bring it about, even at cost to myself.

How do we apply this lesson today? In many ways, Paul's discussion of these rules inverts the common understanding of "strong in faith" and "weak in faith" I have encountered. Usually, it is the person whose faith results in a very religious approach to many matters who is considered the "strong," while the one who is less regulated in his behavior and seems willing to engage in "questionable" behavior who is considered the "weak." These "strong" often view it as their responsibility to guide the "weak" away from this behavior towards their "strength," or to separate themselves from those who will not do so. This can make it difficult to apply the passage properly. After all, is it not the responsibility of the righteous to root out "questionable" behavior? Are we not commanded to "abstain from all appearance of evil" (1 Thess 5:22)?

The thing about "questionable" behavior is that it rarely is questionable to the one who objects or to the one who does not. It is only when they get together that the question arises. The weak believer has likely read enough of the Old Testament to know that God hates idolatry. If that was formerly part of his life, his repentance in Christ likely drives him as far from it as he can get. On the other hand, the strong believer knows the idol is actually nothing, knows that he is not worshiping when he buys meat in the market, and likely does not give it a thought. It is not unusual for the weak to consider the strong wanton or the strong to consider the weak judgmental, precisely because each is "fully persuaded in his own mind."

I was recently asked by a Christian institution what my position was regarding seeing movies "rated higher than PG-13." I responded that I rarely consider the ratings of movies at all these days. The MPAA, which rates movies, is not concerned about the same things that I am. It is concerned with minor details of content, such as someone dragging on a cigarette or word W being used 7 as opposed to 5 times, more than themes and innuendo. If I start a movie and it is offensive trash, I turn it off regardless of and often without ever seeing the rating. At the same time, I do not doubt that there are believers whose consciences genuinely would not permit them to freely watch a movie that was rated R, at least in its original, unedited form. Or, some will not see a movie in the theater at all. An older lady I often visited in a former pastorate had forsworn movie theaters years before. I would think the soap operas or daytime talk shows I often saw on her TV were of less value than many movies, but her commitment was what it was.

How, then, do we love one another? In this instance, I am the strong believer and my counterpart is weak. I am not to think less of him for his conscience. I am not to try to cajole, coerce, or invite him to violate his conscience. I am not to tout a movie as excellent and then say, "Oh, wait. It is R. You cannot watch it because of your silly rule." For his part, my weak brother is not to condemn me or think less of me for my disregard of ratings, if he finds out about it.

Now, this is just one contemporary example of this sort

of issue. There are many. I do not mind rock-ish music in church. The syncopated rhythm has yet to have any wicked effect on me that I have noticed. But, I will not be raising my hands during church music. It would be for show, since it is inadequate to express my true feelings. For that, I would have to dance, and nobody wants that to happen. That is, nobody wants me to dance. Dancing itself has both good and bad forms, I would say. I read from all sorts of Bible versions, but if a church prefers for me to teach from the King James, that just happens to be one of the ones I use. In all of these things I am "fully persuaded." I know the sins that tempt me, and these points do not touch on them.

"Withstood Him to His Face"

Some may still wonder whether Paul's commands to the strong to respect the consciences of the weak should not be extended to everyone who has a qualm about a specific "questionable" behavior. That is, maybe the person who says God forbids me to watch *Baywatch*, when it is only good taste that does so, should be listened to even when he would never watch *Baywatch* and his walk is not at all threatened by my watching it. Is it not loving to give up this program for him?

The answer is no, and for a very important reason. At a certain point the denial of Christian liberty amounts to a denial of the gospel itself. Consider the two situations Paul relates in Galatians 2. When he returned to Jerusalem with Titus, a Greek believer, he rejected all efforts by those who would deny Christian liberty, whom Paul calls "false brothers" (v. 4), to compel Titus to be circumcised. Paul would not submit to their intent, "not, not for an hour; that the truth of the gospel might continue with you" (v. 5). Similarly, Peter had been in the habit in Antioch of eating with Gentiles. But, when certain believers came from James, from Jerusalem, Peter stopped eating with the Gentile believers and "separated himself," prompting even Barnabas to do the same. At this point Paul "withstood him to the face, because he was to be blamed" (v. 11).

Now some might say that this response was so strong because the issues of circumcision and table fellowship were rooted in the distinction between Jews and Gentiles. This was a racial issue, and one has to stand up against racism in the church. This is certainly true, but it is not where Paul takes the justification for his adamancy in these matters. He says that the need to repudiate Jewish distinctives being imposed upon Gentiles is rooted in "knowing that a man is not justified by the works of law, but by the faith of Jesus Christ . . . I do not frustrate the grace of God: for if righteousness is by law, then Christ is dead in vain" (vv. 16, 21). Note that it is not "the law," but simply, "law."[8] Paul is not arguing specifically about the Mosaic statutes. He is arguing against the whole notion that certain behaviors justify. At some point, those who seek to impose their standards on others are threatening the gospel.

---

[8] Despite some English translations, the Greek here is anarthrous; that is, it lacks the article "the."

"Commandments of Men"

But some will say, and quite rightly, that believers cannot just permit any sort of behavior, or pretend that just any sort of behavior is acceptable. Paul rebukes the Corinthian church for boasting, perhaps in the name of grace, of accepting a man's incestuous sexual relationship with his stepmother (1 Cor 5:1-6). Jesus speaks of the need to confront sin and, if necessary, treat the sinner as if he were not a Christian (Matt 18:15-20). It is not up to each of us to call himself "strong" and make up his own rules.

Love does require rebuke at times, as we will see in later chapters. But it also requires not rebuking in some matters, even matters which might seem very important, such as eating meat which is offered to idols. The Jerusalem Council, as recorded in Acts 15, instructed the Gentile churches to abstain from such meat; it was obviously important to them. How, then, do we draw the line?

The answer is, I would suggest, found in the rebuke of Jesus to the Pharisees, of whom he says, "In vain they do worship me, teaching for doctrines the commandments of men" (Matt 15:9). He says this in precisely a discussion of his disciples violating a rule that was important to the Pharisees, that of washing hands before eating. Now, to be fair to the Pharisees, God had given Israel lots of rules about washing in the Mosaic Law; in Exodus through Deuteronomy, forms of "wash" appear in 60 verses. It does not seem unreasonable to extend these rules from God in such a basic and practical way. But Jesus' response makes the point that such extensions, even if reasonable, are not binding in the same way that God's commands are. He does point out that this particular extension misses the point of the Old Testament washing regulations, which were meant to highlight man's need to be cleansed from his own impurities before God. They were not to guard man against external defilement. But the fault of this particular tradition should not obscure the real line Jesus draws, that between what God has commanded and what men believe is best. The former is certain and binding, the latter is not.

There are many things that God has clearly declared to be wrong. They are wrong. But there are many things, even things closely related to what God has declared to be wrong, which He has not declared to be wrong. In these matters Christians have freedom to do as each is fully persuaded, but with the weak loving the strong and the strong loving the weak so that in these areas of freedom they do not harm either. It is absolutely loving to rebuke a fellow believer for violating the command of God. But it is not loving to rebuke a believer for violating what is not the express command of God. In such matters we might seek to convince or persuade our brothers, but we should never act, in thought or in deed, as if violating our take on the wise course is the same as violating the express command of God.

None of this is to suggest, by the way, that bodies of believers, whether local churches or other Christian institutions, cannot and even should not expand upon the rules which God has clearly stated to affirm the community's shared values. But members of such bodies should be careful not to forget that this is what they have done. They have said, "This is our stance. This is how we believe it is best to live out what

God has said." But that is not grounds for thinking less of those who disagree, whether as weak or as strong. For example, in the American south, many Baptist churches articulate a complete rejection of the social drinking of alcohol. I think there are good cultural and biblical reasons for such a position. But such a position goes beyond what God has specifically commanded regarding alcohol. He has forbidden drunkenness and warns about the dangers of alcohol consumption, but even under the Mosaic Law, He permits the drinking of "strong drink" as part of the tithe meal (Deut 14:26). A church that holds such a position should hold it with humility, recognizing that while it is their commitment to communicate their faith, it is nevertheless a tradition of man, not a commandment of God. It would violate the command to love to think ill of a brother because of his conscientious choices regarding alcohol,[9] whether strong or weak.

And this is, remember, what Jesus said would be our most powerful witness. Jesus never said his disciples would be known by their perfect morality. He never said all men would recognize his disciples by their teetotaling or by the fact that they wore suits to mow the grass. If asceticism were the test for Christians, many who had never heard the name of Christ would prove better Christians. But it is not the test. Loving one another is.

We all have to make decisions about other people, and so it is important that we do so lovingly. This means, first, that we

---

[9] Of course, none of this is a shield for drunkenness. On this God has spoken clearly and consistently (e.g., Eph 5:18).

make decisions based upon investigation into the truth. Second, we need to be careful to conduct the investigation in a loving manner, thinking of how we would like someone else to check into us. Third, we need to remember that our decisions should be based upon the clear commands of God, not our own personal preferences about how to best live out those commands. We can judge; indeed, we have to judge. But we can do it lovingly. By this, we will be known as Christ's disciples.

Reflection Questions

1. Would Paul classify you as a "weak" believer or a "strong" one?

2. In your experience, are people who are disturbed by how others behave in matters of conscience more likely to present themselves as authorities to be obeyed, or as genuinely struggling with their own walks?

3. Is there any part of your walk in matters of conscience which is hurting other believers? Does your strength hurt anyone weak with whom you associate? Does your weakness lead you to condemn those who are strong?

"If Thy Brother Shall Trespass"

In the last chapter, we considered how to properly judge, how to properly evaluate, those around us. Loving them means judging them properly, investigating the situation thoroughly to determine the truth. This chapter will look at what we should do when we determine that sin has really been committed. What is the loving way to deal with sin?

"Love Covers a Multitude of Iniquity"

One option when the sin has been committed against you is to simply overlook it. The Preacher of Ecclesiastes says, "Also take no heed unto all words that are spoken; lest thou hear thy servant curse thee: For oftentimes also thine own heart knoweth that thou thyself likewise hast cursed others" (Eccl 7:21-22). While individual verses in the Preacher's search for wisdom may be suspect, this verse seems to spell out an application of 1 Peter 4:8, "And above all things have fervent charity among yourselves: for charity shall cover the multitude of sins." Charity, which is a common translation for "love," sometimes leads us to just cover over sin. Now this is, again, when you find out about a sin against you. Simply covering over or ignoring a sin against another is not something that you can lovingly decide to do.

This is because choosing to ignore a sin against you is a sacrifice, a cost to yourself. You cannot pay that cost for someone else, but you can pay it for yourself. You can forgo your right to justice, to a confrontation, to an apology, to restitution, or whatever you deserve. You might look at someone who has, as the Preacher mentions, said something ugly about you and decide this is something that you are willing to let go. While letting things slide may sound simple and easy enough, it is not always so.

I am reminded of a young man I tutored in math. During his early teen years, he experienced a relatively rapid transition to an adult male physique and ended up on the football team. I remember he was concerned at the start of one tutoring session because of something that had happened in the locker room. Another young man had spoken to him with clear disrespect and acted in a physically threatening manner and he had, because of his Christian beliefs, simply let the matter go. He was concerned, though, that by not confronting this challenge he had "lost face" with the team. Not only was this embarrassing in itself, but it might encourage similar behavior towards him in the future, perhaps now by other members of the team who might perceive his loving abdication of his rights as weakness. I assured him this was not likely. Most people recognize and respect self-control in those with whom they associate, even if they do not practice it themselves. And, I pointed out he had the option, if it came to it another time, to respond differently. But, in the meantime, he had shown moral strength in letting this slide without response or retaliation. This was a loving action on his part, notwithstanding his second thoughts. Indeed, his second thoughts show that this was a genuinely loving decision. He had not ignored this slight because it did not matter to him. He had ignored it despite it being, clearly, important to him.

Of course sometimes we let things go because we really do not care. Or, we might care, but not enough to make the effort or face the discomfort of confronting someone over wrongdoing. We should be careful about covering over sin in these situations. As we will look at in a moment, rebuke is as much a part of love as is covering iniquity. So, what might guide our decision to properly let love cover over iniquity?

First, we should consider the extent to which we are the focus of the sinful act. That is, if a person says something bad about me or disrespects me or takes revenge on me, it might be appropriate to let love cover the matter over. Another way to look at this is to consider what I am actually concerned about. Am I concerned about justice or about the fact that I have been wronged? Second, we should consider the extent to which the offensive action occurred on the spur of the moment or was done in the heat of anger. As the Preacher implies above, we all have behaved badly at such times. Someone sitting calmly who, after careful thought, says something hateful about you likely merits a different response than someone who says the same thing the moment you pinch his finger under the piano you are carrying together. Third, we should consider whether we are actually able to let the sin go. Sometimes, especially in close relationships, we get in the habit of covering over sin. But sometimes even a close loved one crosses a line we cannot honestly overlook. In such cases, pretending everything is okay and that the sin is covered over, when in fact it remains a potential root of bitterness or conflict, is a problem.

Once, while a youth director chaperoning my group at a youth camp, I took a toad I had found on the grounds and carried it in my palm into our cabin for the nightly devotional. One of my young men, call him Todd, was giving the devotional that night. About 10 minutes into it, when I suppose he was about halfway through, one of the young ladies in the group saw the harmless little toad and threw quite the fit. It was apparently contagious and in a moment several girls were freaking out. Needless to say, while it was quite funny, it ruined the young man's devotional. I apologized, not considering the matter particularly serious, and he claimed to accept my apology. Now, this was not exactly the same situation we are discussing, as I did acknowledge my poor decision. However, I found out a couple years later that my action still bothered him. A minor thing done without a hint of malice was still in his mind harming our relationship. We should not let an offense fester in this way under the pretense of love. As Paul says in Eph 4:26, "Let not the sun go down on your wrath." In some cases, rebuke is necessary.

"Faithful are the Wounds"

Many people will do almost anything to avoid confrontation, especially confrontation to rebuke another. Perhaps the only thing harder than going to someone to apologize is to go to someone to reprove him. For the most part, we do not want to be rebuked. For the most part, we respond poorly when we are. The typical believer has no more interest in rebuking his brother than his brother has in being rebuked. Telling another that he has done wrong is often viewed as unkind. And, since I would not like to be rebuked,

I ought not to rebuke another. Doing so would violate the Golden Rule. Doing so would not be loving.

This is one of the times when we must rely upon the wisdom of God, not our personal preferences, to determine what is loving. And God paints a very different picture of what it means to rebuke. God says, "Open rebuke *is* better than secret love. Faithful *are* the wounds of a friend; but the kisses of an enemy *are* deceitful" (Prov 27:5). These final words cannot but bring to mind the betrayal of Jesus by Judas. Judas comes to Jesus by night and greets him with a kiss, thereby identifying him to the mob. This kiss, this greeting meant to show love and close affection, instead is a sign to lead to Jesus' arrest. It is a symbol that does not just lack substance; it means the exact opposite of what it is supposed to convey. Sure, we might want the kiss, might want the friendly greeting. But such a greeting that comes from someone that does not actually mean us well is a lie.

On the other hand, the one who rebukes his brother, when such rebuke is fitting, is showing faithful friendship. He is doing the difficult thing, taking on the unpleasant task and genuine risk that rebuke brings. A man who rebukes his fellow knows all the risks he faces. He risks losing a friend. He risks ridicule for being the narc, the square, the dork, or whatever the current language used to demean the one who upholds standards happens to be. He risks seeing all his errors of the past brought up and thrown into his face, along with perhaps the word, "hypocrite." And, he risks all of this for little, if any, benefit to himself. Most of the time, the things we hesitate to confront our brother about are things that have little bearing on us. They are his issues.

When we perform any act of love, we are of course following God, who Himself is love. And, this is the case when we consider the responsibility to rebuke. Proverbs indicates that God's correction is the sure sign of His love: "My son, despise not the chastening of the LORD; neither be weary of his correction: For whom the LORD loveth he correcteth; even as a father the son in whom he delighteth" (Prov 3:11-12). Hebrews expands on this by fleshing out the inverse, "But if ye be without chastisement, whereof all are partakers, then are ye bastards, and not sons" (Heb 12:8). This is true because the "reproofs of instruction are the way of life" (Prov 6:23). Now, of course, we are not God. We should not view disciplining other believers to be our task; our task is loving, of which rebuke is an occasional, regrettable, yet unavoidable part.

One reason that rebuke is often considered unkind is that it is often viewed as an end in itself. What did you do when your Christian brother sinned against you? I rebuked him. That does not sound very good. Perhaps a better way of saying and thinking about the same thing would be to answer, "I worked to restore him." That is what rebuking is. Rebuking is the tool and means of restoration. Imagine as a parallel a pediatrician who comes home after work and has dinner with a couple of friends. One of them asks him, "So, what did you do today?" The physician might answer either, "I stabbed several children," or, "I vaccinated several children," and be telling the truth either way. But the first answer focuses on the means, the second the end. While it is not always the case that the end justifies the means, it should be acknowledged that the end does justify the means when three things are true: first, when the means is not prohibited by God; second, when the good of the end is greater than the unpleasantness of the means; third, when the means is the only or best way to bring about the end.[10]

So a biblical rebuke, a rebuke that shows true Christian love, is one that is directed at an end beyond itself, and that end is restoration and correction. A Christian who rebukes for the sake of rebuking is like a physician using needles just for the sake of doing so; he is mistaken about his calling. Rebuke that leads to restoration, on the other hand, is part of the edifying ministry to which believers have been called (Eph 4:12, 16).

"Seventy Times Seven"

Jesus teaches that dealing with a brother who sins against you, assuming that love will not cover this sin, begins with a private confrontation. He says, "If thy brother shall trespass against thee, go and tell him his fault between thee and him alone" (Matt 18:15). The goal here is restoration, "If he shall hear thee, thou hast gained thy brother." Peter questions Jesus, "Lord, how oft shall my brother sin against me, and I forgive him? till seven times?" (Matt 18:21). Jesus' well-known

---

[10]That God has in fact commanded rebuke at times makes clear that it is right. I include this reasoning here only to show that thinking about ends and means in rebuking is consistent with how we should think about these things in other matters.

response, "until seventy times seven," suggests that there is no limit to how often a believer forgives another. However, Jesus' words about forgiveness say something about forgiveness that is often neglected. If I truly forgive someone, I must put him in a position from which he can sin against me again. How else could he require the other four hundred and eighty-nine forgivings?

Most Christians do not have trouble with the idea of forgiving, or even saying they forgive. But by this they often mean something like, "I will not try to kill you, but I will let everyone know how badly you wronged me and how kind it was for me to forgive you." Or, perhaps, "I will not bring this up again and try not to think of it, but only on the condition that you leave me alone forever." This is, however, not Christian forgiveness. It is certainly not the forgiveness Christ gives to those he loves. Jesus did not say to Peter, after Peter had denied him three times, "I will not damn you, but do not ever come near me again." No, Jesus walked with Peter, ate with Peter, and gave Peter a vital task in ministry. This is true restoration, and true restoration, restoration that makes one vulnerable to sin again, is much harder. And it is his love for us which is the bar for our love for one another.

Imagine that you invite me over to dinner and, after I have left, notice that some of your silverware is missing. You confront me, and I confess my sin, express regret, and return your silverware. You might say, "I forgive you." But, will you have me over to dinner again? Now, let us imagine that you do have me over to dinner again. And, I steal some of your silverware again. You confront me the next day and I confess my sin, express regret, and return your silverware. Will you forgive me again? Will you have me over to dinner again? And what about the three-hundredth time you have me over and I steal your silverware? Will you once again accept my confession, forgive, and restore me? This is almost unthinkable, but this is what Jesus commanded.

You may be thinking, "There is no way this is what Jesus meant." But let us return again to the nature of love, treating others as well as, indeed better, than you would like to be treated. When you wrong someone and you know it and you confess to them, is not your desire, "Can we forget that this ever happened"? Now, of course, memory is not something over which we have direct control. I remember things I would not mind forgetting and forget things I would like to remember. But the core of the desire is for restoration, for a resetting to things the way they were before the sin was committed. And, if we really do that, then this includes resetting the sinned-against counter to "0." There is, in that sense, no way my brother can sin against me and confess repeatedly. Each time he confesses we start over, because that is how I want to be treated.

I once was discussing my pilfering of silverware with some college students and one suggested that he might have me back over, but he would lock his silverware away. This is a perfectly understandable response, but hardly the way that Christ loves believers. However often we fail him, he does not wall parts of himself away from us. He does not guard himself against our iniquities. He casts our sins into the sea (Micah 7:19) and remembers them no more (Heb 8:12). God is perfectly holy and has a perfect memory. He has a better reason to hold a grudge and a better mind in which to hold it. Yet He is willing to forget that the sins of His people have ever happened. If we are to love one another as Christ loves us, we cannot do less.

There is no more powerful example of this, of risking oneself despite being repeatedly sinned against, than David. He found himself the servant of king Saul, playing his harp to soothe the troubled king. Saul, jealous of David, cast a javelin at David to strike him to the wall and kill him. David "avoided out of his presence twice" (1 Sam 18:11). Later, after David has married Saul's daughter Michal, Saul again throws his javelin at David and David again escapes (1 Sam 19:9-10). It is only when Saul sends men to watch David at home and Michal warns him that Saul will certainly kill him that he flees. And even then, he refused, despite the urging of his men, to harm Saul to protect himself. But those first two times, when David went back to play the harp for the king with the hole, if not a javelin itself, still visible in the wall, are a particularly dramatic testimony to David's love, faith, and commitment.

"He that Covereth a Transgression"

More could be said about how to lovingly deal with those who sin against us. Matthew 18 actually spells out a full procedure for how to do so in the context of the church. However, this is a book more about personal ethics than church discipline. But a final point that should be raised is that of discretion.

As noted above, it is good for believers to cover over sins entirely, when they can properly do so in love. Not every sin against us personally needs to receive our full attention. But even when a sin needs to be dealt with by confrontation and restoration, discretion both during and after the confrontation are appropriate. The circle of those who know about the sin should be as small as possible to still successfully confront it and bring restoration. After restoration is accomplished, the sin should not be mentioned again.

Reflection Questions

1. How and why do you think David did what he did, when he went back to serve Saul after Saul tried to kill him?

2. Which do you think it is easier for you to do, to rebuke or to forgive? Why?

3. What is the worst thing you have ever forgiven? Is there anything you have not forgiven that you should have?

"Leave There Thy Gift Before the Altar"

God, particularly as He has revealed Himself in Christ, is our model for how we love one another. Yet there is one way in which we are required to be loving in which God is not. Unlike God, who always and only does what is right, we wrong one another. And, when we do, we have an obligation to seek forgiveness and reconciliation.

Jesus spoke of this obligation in the Sermon on the Mount. "If thou bring thy gift to the altar, and there remember that thy brother hath ought against thee; leave there thy gift before the altar, and go thy way. First be reconciled to thy brother, and then come and offer thy gift" (Matt 5:23-24). It is important to note the priority which Jesus assigns to this obligation. The "altar" spoken of here is the altar in Jerusalem. An Israelite might have traveled days from the far reaches of the nation to bring his gift to that altar. Yet Jesus suggests that, even as he is standing in the Temple, a man who remembers that his brother has something against him should leave the altar and deal with the one he has wronged. This is potentially quite the round trip. This suggests either that proper relations among His people are more important to God than offerings, that a believer who has sinned against his brother and not dealt with it cannot worship Him properly, or both. Whichever is the case, God is very concerned that a believer who sins against another be reconciled. While reconciliation is in part up to the one who is sinned against, the one who sins should do his part to seek it. Biblically, this involves confession, repentance, and restitution.[11]

"We Acknowledge Our Wickedness"

Biblical reconciliation begins with confession. This is acknowledging that one has, in fact, sinned against another. In Hosea 5:15, God says He will leave Israel to themselves until they "acknowledge their offence." God commands the nation to acknowledge that their idolatry was sin (Jer 3:13), after which he will return them to Zion and provide for them.

In our culture, the apology has come to replace the confession. While sometimes apology is just used as another word for confession, at other times the original meaning of apology creeps into what we do when we should be confessing. Originally, an apology was a defense. Justin Martyr, for example, wrote two books that argued that the Roman state should not persecute Christians titled *apologia*, or apologies. Far from confessing that Christians had sinned against the state, they argued that Christians had done nothing wrong. They did not acknowledge that behavior was wrong, but sought to justify and explain that behavior was right. While there are certainly times when such a defense is appropriate, that sort of apology is not a confession.

---

[11]While this book is about believers loving one another, it is important to recognize that sin is first and foremost against God (Psalm 51:4). Confession and repentance towards God should precede or coincide with reconciling with one's fellow believer.

An apology of this sort is often used appropriately when one accidentally inflicts harm or discomfort on another. For example, if one had picked a can up off the shelf in the grocery store, put it back, and suddenly stepped back onto a lady's toe, such an apology, including an expression of sorrow or displeasure, would be appropriate. "Oh, I'm sorry I stepped on your toe. I stepped back without looking. Are you okay?" While this acknowledges that a regrettable incident occurred, this denies any intentional wrongdoing. This is not a confession, though in this situation a confession is not warranted. Accidents happen. They are not sins.

Now, imagine that Tom and Jane, siblings, are talking and get into an argument. Jane walks to her room, puts on a pair of cowboy boots, comes back out into the living room, and stomps on Tom's toe with the heel of her boot. She then responds, "Oh, I'm sorry I stepped on your toe. You were being a jerk. Are you okay?" This is again not a confession. But in this situation a confession is warranted. Jane intentionally tried to harm Tom without adequate justification. This is a sin and needs to be acknowledged so that Tom and Jane can restore their relationship.

"He that Confesses and Forsakes"

While a youth pastor, one of my young men, Scott, told me he was going to skip out on attending a youth summer mission camp one year. He did not have a reason in particular; he just was not going to attend. He was sorry, though, he assured me. So, I gave him a gentle punch in the meaty part of his upper arm. It was not hard, of course, and he was a solid guy. Then, I told him I was sorry. Then, I punched him again in the same way. I said, "Sorry," again. Punched again. Was sorry again. Finally, he said, "Stop that!" I said, "Why? I said I was sorry. Why should I do anything different?"

You see, Scott saying he is sorry and then maintaining the same behavior which prompted the "sorry" in the first place is not very consistent. I honestly was not particularly concerned about the trip; we had a good group going even without Scott. But it did concern me that he could think that he should be going, which his "Sorry" expressed, but not amend his behavior to what he thought he should be doing. Such a sorry was a meaningless screen, not a genuine expression of anything.

Biblical confession is presumed to lead to repentance, a turning away from the sin which has been confessed. Proverbs 28:13 reads, "He that covereth his sins shall not prosper: but whoso confesseth and forsaketh them shall have mercy." Confessing and forsaking go together. It is not just acknowledging that a behavior is wrong, is sin, that grounds proper reconciliation. The one who has sinned needs to turn from his sin.

In his first letter to them, Paul rebukes the Corinthian church for several things they are doing wrong, including failing to confront a member who is living in gross immorality. In his second letter, he has to remind them that the only purpose of inflicting sorrow upon one another in confrontation is to prompt repentance. He says they need to forgive the sinful member they made sorry with their discipline (2 Cor 2:6-7) and that he is glad they were sorrowful when they received his letter, but:

> not that ye were made sorry, but that ye sorrowed to repentance: for ye were made sorry after a godly manner, that ye might receive damage by us in nothing. For godly sorrow worketh repentance to salvation not to be repented of: but the sorrow of the world worketh death. For behold this selfsame thing, that ye sorrowed after a godly sort, what carefulness it wrought in you, yea, what clearing of yourselves, yea, what indignation, yea, what fear, yea, what vehement desire, yea, what zeal, yea, what revenge! In all things ye have approved yourselves to be clear in this matter (2 Cor 7:9-11).

We should sorrow over our sins, but only to the point that it drives us to repentance.

This need to turn, though, runs up against the very real problem of our fallenness. The man who has indulged losing his temper for 20 years may not successfully turn from this habit in one try or two. The woman who has gossiped in the past may find indiscreet words "just slipping out" before she even really notices. These lapses do not invalidate the reality of the prior confession or effort to forsake. We need to be careful to resist the temptation to get discouraged in such situations, whether we are the sinner or the one sinned against. Jesus recognized that a brother may sin against another many times (Matt 18:22).

Earlier, it was noted that a confession which turns into a defense is not really a confession. Here, it should be noted that a confession followed by a denial of the possibility of change is not really repentance. "I'm sorry I lost my temper. I shouldn't have. But, that is just how I am," is not repenting. The confession which sounds more like self-pity, "I am sorry

I always do everything wrong," is not repentance. There is no ground here for restoration. Worse, the Christian who says this is denying the power of God to change him and conform him to the image of the Son. Jesus did not lose his temper with people inappropriately. He did not sin against them when he did become angry. He did not sin at all. Since God's prearranged destination for each believer is conformity to the image of Christ (Rom 8:29), there is no sin which God intends to remain in the lives of His people. While it is wise for the believer to be aware that he does not have the power, within himself, to change into a good person, it is important that he be open, indeed eager, for God to change him.

As part of this willingness to change, we should be ready to take extra precautions to set up walls against the sin from which we intend to turn. The person who is prone to gossip sometimes just needs to slow down all conversation, to suppress the urge to speak at every opportunity. The person who is turning from adultery needs to avoid contact with anyone who has engaged in this behavior with him or anyone with whom he might be tempted to commit it again. True repentance involves moving away from sin.

"Restore Five Oxen for an Ox"

We do not hear much about restitution today, particularly not in the personal lives of believers. However, the Mosaic Law makes numerous references to restitution. Leviticus 24:18 presents the simplest form of this, "He that killeth a beast, he shall restore it." Other laws of restitution add a premium on top of that which is taken, such as Leviticus 6:2, which adds a fifth to what one restores who has sworn a false oath, or Exodus 22:1, "If a man steal an ox, or a sheep, and kill it, or sell it; he shall restore five oxen for an ox, and four sheep for a sheep." There is some tension among the various specifics, but the basic principle of restitution is consistent.

Is restitution consistent with forgiveness? The Mosaic Law presents them as distinct events that can occur together. For example, in Leviticus 6:5-7, the one who added a fifth in restitution was still to make a trespass offering. This offering is an atonement which is connected to his relationship with the Lord. Restitution does not buy forgiveness, and forgiveness does not remove the need for restitution.

This is the case because the sin which needs to be forgiven is not the same as the loss which the victim suffers. There are lots of ways in which you might lose your silverware. Your house might burn down or there might be a tsunami. The sin involved if I steal your silverware is not your losing them, but my betraying you, my violating your trust and your right to possess your property in safety. That is the wrong I do to you and the harm I do to our relationship. Forgiving me that wrong is entirely separate from you no longer having your silverware. Paul addresses this distinction when he discusses his rebuke of the Corinthians and their consequent sorrow. He says he did not rebuke them because he was overly concerned about the specific sin being committed but because of the nature of their relationship (2 Cor 7:12). Likewise, forgiving me when I steal your silverware is about our relationship; your silverware is another matter. And in these other matters, these vehicles by which we sin against one another, it is important that we seek to make restitution.

Restoration is the act of the offended to return the offender to the prior relationship. Restitution is the effort of the offender to return the offended to his prior condition. For example, if the offender has damaged the offended's reputation with gossip, particularly false gossip, restitution involves speaking to those who heard the original tale to restore that reputation. In such cases, the retraction should be more prominent than the original gossip. If the offender has cost the offended a job, restitution would involve seeking to find the offended a job and perhaps making provision for the offended until he is employed again. Restitution means that the offended should not bear the consequences of the offender's sin. Of course, in some instances restitution is impossible; some things cannot be replaced or repaired. But the one who truly loves the one against whom he has sinned will seek to remove, as much as possible, the effects of sin from its victim.

Is This Loving?

In my experience, many people seem very uncomfortable hearing a confession, not in the sacramental sense, but in the sense of personally hearing someone say, "I was wrong to do that to you. I ask you to please forgive me." People will sometimes attempt to deny that such a confession is necessary, either by downplaying the sin or by attempting to provide some extenuating circumstances. I once, as an adult, had done something inconsiderate to my father. I went to him and acknowledged that I had and that I was wrong and he took the conversation the other way, emphasizing how wrong I was. I acknowledged he was right, but his first impulse was not to really hear the confession. And these are just responses to the words; efforts at restitution can provoke even stronger resistance.

Given that such open and full confession seems to make people uncomfortable, is it really the loving thing to do? There is good reason to believe that it is. First, God commands it, and, as we have noted before, He and His commands are our standard for love. Second, if we consider what we really want for ourselves, so that we might do it unto others, do we not really want for those who wrong us to confess? Certainly, we are trained in our culture to not believe in a right side or, by extension, a wrong side. People have a "falling out"; it is not as if one sinned against the other. Marriages end through "no fault"; there is just divorce. There are two sides to every story, and neither is particularly right or wrong. But confession breaks all that apart. And this explains why it both is loving and does make people uncomfortable. We do sometimes want to be vindicated in our own minds that we have been wronged and that it was not some neutral exchange in which everyone is wrong. And there is nothing wrong with wanting that; it is the truth.

But beyond this, hearing a confession brings one to a point of decision. It means the one wronged no longer can simply be the one wronged. He has to make a decision whether to restore the relationship or not. If he is a Christian, it brings his obligation to forgive fully home in an unavoidable way. The responsibility for the future of the relationship is now his.

It also puts him in the position of reflecting on his own behavior. He now knows he has been wronged, but he may have wronged as well. Confession can be an unpleasant reminder of one's own responsibility.

Despite this unpleasantness, confession is needed to "clear the air" in relationships. Proper relationships cannot be built on a confusing mass of unresolved sin and resentment. Recall the story of David and Absalom. Absalom had killed his brother and David neither fully restored Absalom nor executed justice upon him. Their relationship was marred by the absence of both true confession and complete forgiveness, and that dysfunction led to a revolt which harmed the entire nation of Israel. That is not a relationship of love.

Unfortunately, that is how the world presents relationships to us today. I think of the soap operas that were on in the house when I was a child. I cannot remember many specific plotlines or stories, but I do recall the mass of deceit and betrayal and unresolved conflicts. Much of primetime television today appears, at least from the previews, to tell the same sorts of stories. Even people in the closest relationships, spouses, siblings, and parents, see their relationships marred by unconfessed sin. Certainly, television is not life, but the stories it tells both are shaped by and shape life. If Christians are to be known by their love for one another, a love that sets them visibly apart from the world, their relationships simply cannot be the same as those found in the world. They must be characterized by loving confession and forgiveness.

Reflection Questions

1. Is there anything in your life which you should confess to a fellow believer? Is there anything for which you have apologized that really merits a confession?

2. Do you think it is hard to restore the one who confesses to your prior relationship? Why?

3. What is your experience with restitution? Have you ever received a real confession and still felt hollow because restitution was not made? Have you ever been offered restitution and not felt comfortable with it? Have you ever heard it preached upon?

"More than 120,000 Persons"

Much of the Old Testament focuses on God's covenant relationship with Israel. He loves Israel, but not because of any greatness within the nation itself (Deut 7:7-9). He is faithful to them, though they often fail Him. He looks out for them and delivers them from many evils. His love for them is an everlasting one (Jer 31:3).

Yet God's love for Israel does not always result in Him doing what is pleasant for them. At times, their sins incur His judgment, loving though it may be. At other times, however, something else intrudes upon Him giving Israel, whom He loves, what they would desire. That something else is His love for others.

In the book of Jonah, God sends a reluctant prophet to threaten judgment upon Nineveh. Like all threats, its purpose is to not be fulfilled. Just as a father threatens his son with consequences if he hits his sister precisely so he will never have to deal out those consequences, so God threatens Nineveh with judgment precisely so He will not have to judge them. Jonah knows this and so flees rather than delivering Nineveh the threat (Jonah 4:2). Yet God makes certain that Jonah does deliver His message and, in the face of Nineveh's repentance, relents. Yet Jonah remains, overlooking Nineveh, to see what becomes of it.

Jonah has every reason to despise Nineveh. It is the capital of Assyria, a power which was a historic enemy and oppressor of Israel. It is unclear when in the rise of Assyria's power this story takes place, but the animosity between the nations is clear. God certainly knows that Assyria will soon destroy the Northern Kingdom of Israel and carry many of the people, people of the nation which He loves, away into captivity. Destroying Nineveh is something the wicked city deserves. It is something that would help protect the nation He loves. It is something that would please Jonah, His prophet. Yet destroying Nineveh is not what God does. And the reason He gives is that there are other people involved: "Should I not have compassion on Nineveh, the great city in which there are more than 120,000 persons?" (Jonah 4:11).

As defined earlier, love is the desire for the highest good of another that moves one to act, even at expense to himself, to bring about that good. This is a solid definition, but it addresses love primarily in terms of two people, the lover and the loved. Life is often more complicated than that. As I write this and hope to write something of benefit to you who read it, there are other people in both our lives. Consider my wife and children. The time I spend writing this is time I am not spending with them. And you, as you read this, you are not doing other things that you could be doing. When even a minor choice of something we do means there are many things we are not doing, how do we judge what is the loving choice, the loving thing to do?

It can be difficult to weigh choices that have a large effect on a single person and small effects on many. For example, consider a local raffle. Lots of people buy tickets for $1 each. A ticket number is drawn and one person gets much of the money from the tickets, say, $1000. It seems a great system, in that there is a winner but no losers. That is, it is hard to view the many ticket buyers as losers, when they lose so little, especially compared to the winner. But the reality is that they are losers. An honest and complete evaluation of the situation cannot ignore this.

So, when we think of our responsibility to love one another, we must keep in mind not just the big effects our actions have on the person in front of us, but also the effects our actions have on the many other people affected by them. It might help to illustrate this with an example that we would all agree is wrong. Imagine a security guard in a large department store who sees someone tuck a gold necklace in her purse. He might think it would be loving to ignore what he sees. After all, catching this woman and handing her off to the police will significantly harm, if not outright ruin, her life. Against this, he might weigh the well-being of the store. Certainly, a large business like this could absorb a hundred dollar loss. It could, but it is the way it would do so that would matter. It would either cut costs or increase revenue elsewhere. Cutting costs would mean, most likely, dropping an employee's hours or, perhaps, letting someone go entirely. Or, it could increase revenue by increasing prices. Everything bought at the store for the next few weeks costs an extra 1 cent. Effectively, the original shoplifter is not stealing from the store. She is stealing from all those people who buy the products the prices of which have been inflated to cover her theft. "Loving" her by ignoring her crime means cheating all of them, which does not seem so loving after all.

"I Will Not Offer"

If it can be hard to know, much less weigh, the consequences of how we treat one person, how do we factor this into loving? The answer is found in the part of the original definition of love offered above which said, "at cost to oneself." We love by only giving up what is genuinely ours to give. The security guard mentioned above cannot "lovingly" overlook the theft of the necklace because it is not his necklace. It is not his proper place to give it away. The judge who lets a guilty criminal go, thinking this is love, misunderstands that what he is giving away is not his to give. He is an authority put in place to defend what is yours and mine. To return to David, who sought to halt God's judgment of Jerusalem, it is not love to offer what costs us nothing. We must possess what we are willing to give up in love.

There is a very painful illustration of this that we see in our nation from time to time. On June 17th, 2015, nine people were murdered at the Emanuel African Methodist Episcopal Church in Charleston, South Carolina. Members of the church, including family members of the victims, were very quick to publicly forgive the murderer. To the extent that they meant they would not personally seek vengeance against him, their actions are consistent with biblical commands. However, sometimes people suggest that if the family of a victim forgives a criminal, the criminal should not face justice, or at least not full justice, for his crime. This confuses what is in one person's possession to give. If you steal my family member from me, that loss of mine is mine to forgive. But the nature and value of another human's life is not mine. I do not own or possess it, even if that person is my child. I cannot sacrifice it or give it up and call that love. God connects justice for murder to His image, to His declaration that man is created in His image, like His likeness (cf. Gen 9:6, Gen 1:26). Whatever else we might say about this image, it is not something we own in someone else's life. It is not something we can sacrifice. It is not a vessel for our love.

There are many other examples of people who give away what is not theirs to give. Teachers sometimes give students higher grades than their work merits. Certainly, the student who benefits may be glad. But the grades do not belong to the teacher to give. They involve others over the teacher who set standards. They involve other students who deserve more or less recognition. They involve a community that will look at a transcript and consider the student qualified for certain things on the basis of this grade. All of these others are potentially wronged by the simple act of giving lower quality work a grade higher than it deserves. It costs the teacher nothing, but the community much. Similarly, politicians and government officials take money from person A and give it to person B and call it charity, that is, love. Whether this is proper government policy is one issue, but when Politician Joe takes money from A and gives it to B, he cannot take credit for loving B or being generous with B. He is not sacrificing what is his. When he reaches into his wallet to give money to B, he is being generous. When he reaches into your wallet, he is being something very different.

In the home, it is important for family members to respect what is possessed by each member and not presume to give it up. For example, as an adult Christian man, I believe the proper response to physical violence directed at me because I am me is to turn the other cheek (Matt 5:39).[12] So, if you and I were talking and you got mad at me and punched me, I would, I hope, not respond in kind. However, I teach my children how to defend themselves against physical violence and respond to it effectively. Their ability to defend themselves is not mine to sacrifice on their behalf. I cannot say, "Well, they should turn the other cheek, so I will make sure they do." In fact, by equipping them to respond physically to violence, I give them the real option of acting out Matt 5:39. When a wimp turns the other cheek, he is not loving. He is not giving up anything, because he does not possess any other option. It is for my children, when they are adult believers in Christ, to make their own choices whether to exercise the option to turn the other cheek or not. Similarly, my children's toys, the money I set aside for their provision, their security, their well-being, and so on, are not mine to sacrifice. If someone is in need and comes to me, I should be willing to give up what is mine to assist this person, but I am not to give up what is my wife's or my child's.

When we give up only what is genuinely ours in love, we are able to love both the one and the 120,000. The home is not the only place where one in authority should keep this rule in

---

[12] I distinguish this from violence directed at me by a criminal because he is a criminal. There, I believe the delegated responsibility of the American state to its citizens requires me to act differently.

mind. It is one thing for a pastor to invite a repentant thief over to his house for dinner and risk his flatware. It is another thing for him to give this thief the keys to the church building to host an unsupervised meeting of those the thief met in prison.

"It Is a Gift"

I have spent a couple pages spelling out some things we cannot properly give away and call it love. It is worth raising a caution based upon something the Pharisees did in Jesus' day. In Matt 15:4-5, Jesus rebukes the Pharisees for, when confronted with a mother or father in need, saying they could not aid them because they had dedicated all their possessions to God. Since they were dedicated to God, those possessions were not really available for the Pharisee to give to his parents to meet their needs. Thus the Pharisee evaded the responsibility inherent in the commandment to honor his father and mother.

My goal here is not to give excuses to not love the one for the sake of the 120,000. But a crafty reader can certainly use these words to excuse himself. For example, he can put 100,000, or even 1,000,000, dollars into his child's "college fund" to protect that money from the obligation to love. After all, that is his child's money now.

Telling the truth, though, always raises such risks. The reality is that no text such as this can force someone to follow its goal or intent. But, if your heart is really set on loving your brother, remembering that not everything you have control over is really yours to give away is important. Love includes a willingness to sacrifice, but not everything is yours to sacrifice. As mentioned above, some people have a stronger claim on you and what you control than do others. This is something to remember to be sure our desire to love one does not prompt us to wrong another. It is not something to abuse to cover our desire to not love at all.

Reflection Questions

1. Has someone ever taken it upon himself to give away something of yours? What did you think of that?

2. What sorts of things do you hold in trust for others? Do not just consider material things, but also prerogatives, time, and other intangibles.

3. How conscious are you of the difference between what you hold in trust for others, whether that be material or immaterial, and what is genuinely yours to give away as you please?

"Speaking the Truth in Love"

Jesus is the truth (John 14:6). God's word is truth (John 17:17). The connection between God and truth is consistent throughout the Bible. Telling man the truth is part of why Jesus came, so that we might know the truth and the truth might make us free (John 8:32). It is through God's true word that man is made holy (John 17:19).[13] Thus, as part of the new life in Christ, Christians are commanded to "speak every man truth with his neighbor" (Eph 4:25).

More often than this verse, though, I have heard Ephesians 4:15, which states Christians should be "speaking the truth in love." The idea of speaking the truth is connected to the loving life of a Christian. "In love" occurs 5 times between Ephesians 3:17 and 5:2. But many times 4:15 is brought up not so much to encourage speaking the truth as to qualify this obligation with the need for it to be spoken "lovingly." It is as if Paul were commanding believers to speak the truth in a loving way and, if we cannot speak it in such a way, to be silent.

That this is not, in fact, what Paul or God have in mind is clear from the many times truth-speaking is commended and lying is rebuked in Scripture. Proverbs presents wisdom as inherently truthful in speech (8:7). God laments the

---

[13]This is the means of man's personal, experiential holiness. Man is set apart unto God positionally in Jesus Christ through faith in him.

wickedness of his people because "they will deceive every one his neighbor, and will not speak the truth" (Jer 9:5). James warns against glorying in strife and lying against the truth (3:14). Lying is a deed of the "old man," and should be put off with him (Col 3:9). Thus, "speaking the truth in love" is not a command so much to only speak the truth when one can do it lovingly as it is a recognition that part of love is speaking the truth.

In previous chapters, we have discussed rebuke and confession. Both of these are aspects of speaking the truth about specific occurrences of sin. In this chapter and the next we will consider some broader categories of speaking the truth and the importance of doing so.

Truth about Self

In Acts 5, we read about an early and tragic conspiracy within the Church. The body is young and has needy members. Some of those with property sell their property and give the proceeds to the Apostles to distribute to the needy. A man, "Ananias, with Sapphira his wife" sell some land and give part of the proceeds to the Apostles while representing that they are in fact giving the full price. As a result, they are both convicted in turn of lying to and tempting the Holy Spirit of God and both in turn fall down dead (vv. 1-10).

The meaning of this story in the context of Acts aside, Ananias and Sapphira represent a common flaw in us, and that is the desire to look better than we are. Most of us are inclined to exaggerate our accomplishments and the obstacles we overcome. We minimize our errors and try to distance ourselves from them. We present to people those parts of ourselves most likely to induce others to think of us the way we would prefer. This inclination spans all aspects of our lives: anecdotes, résumés, introductions, dating profiles, scholarship applications, etc. We present to people pictures of ourselves intended to get us what we desire. This is, by definition, rather antithetical to love. And, if we take the example of Ananias and Sapphira seriously, it should be terrifying. While God does not seem to have continued to strike dead everyone who exaggerates his contribution to God's work, the fact that He did so once should make clear His position on the subject.

Thus, we should take care to guard against our natural inclination to gild ourselves and our endeavors, particularly when we are trying to gain favor by such gilding. When chatting with friends a good story can become a great one with a little poetic license, but the same license is not proper when applying for a job or filling out a tax return. Speaking the truth about ourselves includes two elements, speaking when we ought to speak and speaking the truth when we do speak.

There are many truths about ourselves we benefit from keeping to ourselves. My wife and I were once working for a company that was having some problems and was rapidly going downhill. Every week or two, someone was being fired or laid off. We sought and found other employment, but did not let our current employer know that we intended to quit until the day we intended to stop coming. After all, we thought, if we try to give two weeks notice they may just fire us on the spot. While it may have been practical and appropriate to conceal our plans in this case, this was not the sort of love Christians should show to one another. It put my immediate supervisor in something of a bind; my job needed to be done, and I left her with only one day to get a replacement trained.

This is not to suggest that everyone needs or wants to know everything about us. There are biblical grounds for keeping matters private and silent. But two things should govern this silence. First, love for other believers should be the guide here, not love for oneself. For example, consider John, a young Christian who, for whatever reason, comes to find out that he will not be able to have children without miraculous divine intervention. This need not be the opening line of every phone call or even every date John has. But if on a second date he finds that the other participant, Lucy, is eager to have many children once married, this painful truth should come out. Second, when one does speak, one speaks the truth. John should tell the truth. He should not presume to end the relationship in unexplained silence or with a false explanation. These options might spare his feelings, but they will almost certainly hurt Lucy. Worse, they will usurp her choice about how to handle the situation. Perhaps children are not as important to her as was originally suggested. Perhaps she was only saying that because she thought John desired children; something of his problem may have come through in how he spoke of what he believed he would never have. Or perhaps this is a deal-breaker for Lucy; they both must find someone else. Either way, John should speak the truth in love.

When we do speak of ourselves, we should speak truthfully. Why did your last job really end? There is a big difference between being downsized and being fired for cause, even if you disagree with the cause. I am reminded of an episode of *The Simpsons* in which Homer Simpson and some generic extras are at a job interview. One of the questions is, "What do you consider your greatest weakness as an employee?" The other applicants are shown answering variations on the common theme, "I can be something of a workaholic." Homer, on the other hand, lets out a long list of real weaknesses, indicating that he is lazy, tends to sleep on the job, is not very bright, and so on. It is a funny example of a man without guile. Of course, that sort of truthfulness can be very difficult and have unpleasant consequences. But love does mean accepting those consequences upon ourselves so that they do not fall upon others.

Truth about Others

I was recently watching a political debate in which several candidates addressed women in the military. A couple mentioned their own daughters and one said something to the effect, "I tell my daughters they can be anything they want to be." I thought to myself, "What a liar you are." All sorts of children want to be all sorts of things they can never be. They want to be unicorns and fairies, eagles and horses, wizards and knights. A friend of the family who wears a beard was discussing how his young daughter was crushed when she found out she would not be able to be a girl with a full, pink beard. That was what she wanted, but that would never be. It is one thing to encourage the imagination and fantasies of children, to encourage them to follow their passions and see where they take them. It is quite another to give them unrealistic expectations about reality and themselves. My son will never be a 30' tall robot, whatever he might want. My daughter will never be a neutron star.

Unfortunately, telling other people the truth about themselves has fallen not just out of fashion, but into utter disfavor. Telling people unpleasant truths about them is considered rude, judgmental, hateful, oppressive, and so on. Yet part of the truth we speak in love must be to tell people things about them they might not want to hear.

The proof of this is in the example of Jesus. Time and again he confronted people with the cold, hard realities of their limits, their inadequacies, and their needs. To a rich young man who seemed to think he would inherit eternal life by having kept the commandments, Jesus said, "One thing you lack," go, sell all you have, and follow me. And why did he tell him that? Because "Jesus beholding him loved him" (Mark 10:21). Jesus' love prompted him to deliver this painful truth; he was lacking. When some confronted him with horrible deaths suffered by other Jews, Jesus warned them, "Unless you repent, you shall all likewise perish" (Luke 13:3, 5). They needed to repent. Jesus said to some Jews who had to some degree believed in him, "You cannot hear my word. You are of your father the devil" (John 8:31, 43, 44). These Jews had a real problem that kept them from properly hearing him. Jesus did not pretend with these people. He did not build up false hope in them. He spoke the truth in love.

Similarly, we need to be honest with other people about themselves. This is not a suggestion to be constantly offering one's beliefs uninvited; it is only a reminder that when we are speaking to people or answering questions, our loving responsibility is to tell the truth. At its heart, this is a responsibility to share the truth of the gospel. Lost people are doomed to eternal judgment if they do not repent and trust Christ to save them by imputing his atoning death to their account. Similarly, to return to the issue of rebuke, when we see someone claiming the name of Christ and living in open sin, our responsibility is to say, "Friend, I am not your judge. But I want to warn you that, based upon the clear teaching of Scripture, as stated in verses X, Y, and Z, you are not living as a follower of Christ would or should." But even beyond this, even in matters that do not involve sin and salvation, we should be honest with people.

Imagine, for example, that you are a seminary professor. In the second week of an eight-week class, you receive a message from a student, Sarah, requesting extra time on an assignment. She was in the hospital all weekend because her son, Jonah, has been diagnosed with a serious illness. How do you respond? Well, certainly you would inquire after Jonah's health and express your condolences and concern. You might commit to pray. But many times I find such students need a realistic reminder that they may need to drop school for a time to deal with the really important things in life. It would be easy to offer generic assurances and keep the student in the class; after all, Sarah wants to successfully complete the class and people can do anything they want to do, right? Not at all. That is not how life really is.

Of course, we are not God. There are things about people that we do not know. We should be careful about substituting our wisdom for theirs. But I find this to be a far less common problem than the opposite, that of not confronting people with painful realities about themselves.

One area in which our culture is utterly failing in this regard is in how it is dealing with the transgender movement. This is a movement which suggests that those who, at some point in their lives, have a sense that they are not really of the sex to which they are born should or should be allowed to undergo various treatments and surgeries to make their secondary sexual characteristics and their external genitalia conform to the sex with which they desire to identify. The move in America today is to view these procedures as appropriate for people at a younger and younger age. Clearly, there are moral issues involved in this debate, but here I desire only to note the practical truths which love demands in this conversation. First, many people who experience transgender feelings spontaneously cease to do so. Second, many of those who have undergone these procedures regret their decisions to do so later or feel worse about their sexual identity than they did before undergoing them. Third, the suicide rate among those who have undergone these procedures is radically higher than the norm. Fourth, let us consider the relationship life that someone who decides to undergo these procedures will experience. Imagine Sal, a young man who just feels like he is a woman in a man's body. People around him tell him he should transition to female, and he finds a physician who helps him do so as a relatively young man. He takes the necessary hormones and has the surgeries so that those who see him see the body of a woman, and he takes the name Sally. He moves on with his life as if he were a woman. How will Sally connect with people later in life? Despite the physical externalities, he will never be a woman. His cells will forever be marked as XY, male, cells. He cannot conceive or bear children, and thus cannot fill the role of a mother with a man whom he later meets and with whom he wants to form an intimate relationship. Certainly, he might find a man or woman who desires a relationship with a transgender male, but he will never, in his most intimate relationships, be able to maintain the pretense of being a woman. What is being offered him is a lie, that he can become a woman. The reality is that he can add to his internal gender confusion external sexual confusion, at great expense and discomfort. And too many Christians, in the name of love and acceptance, are going along with the lie.

"Take a Heifer with You"

This chapter has discussed the importance of telling the truth to love. Many of these standards have the potential for being very difficult or for having unpleasant consequences for the one who abides by them. So, before closing out the chapter, I wanted to highlight a couple of times when God sanctions the selective telling of the truth.

In 1 Samuel 16, God has rejected Saul as king over Israel. He commands Samuel, his prophet, to anoint a new king, a son of Jesse. Samuel is naturally concerned; Saul will likely kill him rather than allow him to anoint another king. God commands Samuel to take a heifer with him and sacrifice it as cover for the other task of anointing a new king. When the elders of Bethlehem ask Samuel what he is up to, he is able to answer, "I am come to sacrifice unto the LORD" (v. 5) and avoid any risk of Saul's ire. This is the truth, though not the whole truth.

In Jeremiah 37 and 38, Zedekiah the king comes to Jeremiah and seeks his counsel. As part of their conversation, Zedekiah expresses his fear of some of the "princes" among the Jews (38:4). He fears in particular that they will find out what he has asked of Jeremiah and turn against him. So, he instructs Jeremiah to tell these princes, if they ask, that he asked the king not to return him to the prison in the house of Jonathan the scribe, lest he die there (38:26). This is something Jeremiah has requested from the king in the past (37:20), and when the princes ask him about his meeting with the king, it is this very limited portion of the conversation which he acknowledges, as the king had suggested.

In each of these instances the prophet clearly says less than "the whole truth." He is selective about what he says to protect himself, in the case of Samuel, and the king, in the case of Jeremiah. Neither man lies, but both are selective in telling the truth. Since God in fact commands Samuel to do this, this is presumably not sin. The Christian responsibility to speak truthfully thus cannot be accurately construed as a responsibility to always tell the whole truth. While these instances do not override the clear biblical emphasis on truthfulness and honesty, they show that there are instances in which one is not obligated to tell the whole truth. Partial truth, even partial truth which one knows may and believes will lead to misunderstanding, may be all that one should say. If someone is seeking your harm, you are not obligated to provide him the information he needs to or that will encourage him to harm you. We should not press these exceptions to cover up self-interested secretiveness or to validate lying, but we should keep them in mind when the whole truth might harm one we should be concerned about protecting.

Reflection Questions
1. Do you always want to hear the truth? Does that shape how you think of telling the truth to others?

2. Jesus called people children of the devil to their faces. How does that fit with your picture of Jesus, his love, and his words? Does anything need to change about how you think of these things?

3. How confident are you that what the Bible teaches is trustworthy? Does your willingness to speak those truths in love reflect that confidence?

"Abhor Evil, Cleave to Good"

In Romans 12, Paul describes the wondrous body of believers which is formed by God through the gospel he has just fully explicated. Early in this discussion, Paul writes, "Let love be without dissimulation. Abhor that which is evil; cleave to that which is good. Be kindly affectioned one to another with brotherly love." Sandwiched between commands to love is the powerful language, "Abhor evil, cleave to good." Part of loving is abhorring evil. Love which does not abhor evil is, by implication, not love at all. It is feigned love, pretend love, a deceitful pretense of love. It is, as discussed previously, like the kisses of an enemy, soft on the cheek but of no value against the knife he hides behind his back. The love we have for one another must be love that abhors evil.

"Love the sinner, but hate the sin," is a common saying, but the connection between these points is often missed. These are not two separate activities, as if one could love the sinner without hating sin. Many people today see no connection between morality and the well-being of humans. Morals are matters in which narrow-minded, old-fashioned, or otherwise backwards people attempt to limit the behavior of others for no other reason than that it is enjoyable. The God of the Bible is believed to be a cosmic killjoy whose rules exist to oppress or repress humanity. "Bad" behavior is actually better for people, because it is what they enjoy in the moment. Any unwanted consequences are either the fault of the oppressors or able to be avoided through technology or more enlightened attitudes.

This is not at all the biblical picture of what good and evil are. In the Genesis creation account, "good" carries the particular meaning of "beneficial for humanity." While light (1:4) and land (1:10) are called "good," darkness, sea, and sky are not. This is not because these are "evil," but because these are not the environment in which humans thrive. We see better in the light, get wrinkly in the sea, and have the habit of falling out of the sky. Similarly, heavenly bodies by which humans can see and tell time (1:18) and gold which, to my knowledge, only humans use (2:12), are called good.[14] Biblical goodness is not something which benefits God. Indeed, as a holy, transcendent creator, He does not need anything from humans and cannot be benefitted by what they do. As Paul relates in Acts 17:25, God is not "worshipped with men's hands, as though He needed any thing, seeing He gives to all life, and breath, and all things." God does not need man to be good and does not benefit if man is. Man needs to be good precisely because he benefits when he is so.

The reality is that the behavior which the Bible identifies as sin is detrimental to mankind, both individually and as a whole. It has negative consequences. Cultures the world over have recognized this about many of the Bible's commands. "Thou shalt not murder," and, "Thou shalt not steal," for examples, have been codified as law the world over because societies realize, upon any reflection, that having these rules is necessary for the prosperity of that society. And the evidence

---

[14]See also Sailhamer, *The Pentateuch as Narrative*, 84-97.

consistently bears out that the consequences for all behavior which the Bible deems sin are unpleasant consequences. Part of telling the truth in love means letting people know this precisely so that they can amend their behavior and avoid these consequences for themselves and those around them.

Just as we cannot be anything we might wish to be, so we cannot engage in any and every behavior without experiencing unpleasant consequences for ourselves and those around us. Again, Christians have the responsibility of telling those we love the truth in such matters. It is often easier to "mind our own business," but it is rarely loving. Since we are not God, however, we are not always in a position to predict the consequences of behavior with sufficient certainty to warn others. But there is one broad area of behavior in which we can be certain of unpleasant, if not devastating, consequences. That area is sin, and its consequences are damaging to all those touched by it.

For example, there is simply no question in sociology that the intact biological family, in which a mom and a dad raise children whom they have conceived together, is the best living environment for everyone in it. Mom and dad are healthier, wealthier, recover from illness faster, are more satisfied with life, and enjoy a host of other benefits. Children are safer, healthier, grow up to be more stable adults, are less likely to be involved in crime, end up better educated, and so on. There is simply no question about this, and the evidence is available on the internet for anyone who cares to look for it.[15]

Conversely, this means that any willing decision to move away from an intact biological family is a decision to bring relative harm on oneself and those one loves. A woman with children who divorces her husband and gains sole custody of her children, for example, increases the likelihood that her sons will end up in jail. The single best predictor for whether a young man will end up in jail is not race, economic status, or intelligence, but whether or not he grew up with a father in the home. Even if he does not end up in jail, his life is likely to be harder in many ways. And the wife who makes this decision is similarly harmed by it. Divorcees are not suddenly happy, healthy, and prosperous. The Christian support of marriage is not blind moralism, but recognition of the real harm that follows this deviation from the ideal

It is common to respond to facts like this with extreme cases. Should a woman whose husband is abusing her and the

---

[15] I would note that the evidence is not always presented as it in fact is. For example, in a *Scientific American* article reporting on the findings in E. Mavis Hetherington and John Kelly, *For Better or For Worse: Divorce Reconsidered* (W.W. Norton, 2002), the fact that 25% of the children of divorced parents "experienced serious social, emotional or psychological troubles compared with 10 percent of those whose parents remained together," was presented as a minor change, rather than a 150% increase in probability. Hal Arkowitz, Scott O. Lilienfeld, "Is Divorce Bad for Children?"
http://www.scientificamerican.com/article/is-divorce-bad-for-children, accessed Apr 1, 2016.

children stick with him? Certainly, such cases exist and must be addressed honestly. But honestly addressing them does not mean remaining silent about the other side of things. A man who wants to divorce his wife because his secretary is younger needs, among other harsher things, to hear the truth about the consequences of his actions for everyone involved. Yes, there are single mothers who do valiant work to raise their children; this does not make single-motherhood ideal. Decisions to move away from what God has presented as ideal should never be addressed in a way that minimizes the good of God's ideals or the dangers in moving away from them.

Divorce is not the only issue here. One might also speak to the growing acceptance of same-sex relationships within culture and among professing Christians. Much of this acceptance is being offered with no concern about the real consequences of this behavior. AIDS persists in America, despite the minimal media attention it gets today, and continues to afflict predominantly males engaging in sexual activity with other males. While the cultural paradigm is that men abuse women in relationships, the reality is that, among young people surveyed in America from 2001-2009, "dating violence" and forced sexual activity was far more common among those identifying as same-sex than heterosexual, each being reported with almost triple the median frequency.[16]

---

[16] CDC, *Sexual Identiy, Sex of Sexual Contacts, and Helath-Risk Behaviors Among Students in Grades 9-12 – Youth Risk Behavior Surveillance, Selected Sites, United States, 2001-2009*, 9-10.

While the report just cited mixed rather disparate "risk factors" such as not wearing a bicycle helmet, not eating or drinking two servings of fruit juice per day, being a victim of dating violence, and attempting suicide, it still found that students who identified as heterosexual or who engaged in only heterosexual behavior were the least at-risk group across all categories.[17] When the U.S. CDC, not at all a bastion of Christian morality, concludes, "Sexual minority students, particularly gay, lesbian, and bisexual students and students who had sexual contact with both sexes, are more likely to engage in health-risk behaviors than other students,"[18] Christians should be speaking this truth in love to anyone recommending wholesale acceptance and endorsement of this behavior.

The goal here is not to pick out specific behaviors as the worst evils. The point is that love recognizes evil as abhorrent. Evil deserves abhorrence not because of blind obedience to ancient traditions, but because it hurts people. Theft, tyranny, fraud, adultery, malicious thoughts, racial prejudice, and anything else which the Bible identifies as wrong or evil merits our loathing precisely because we love people. My desire for the good of my fellow Christian should prompt me to loathe all evil: mine, his, and that of a third party.

Abhorring evil means, in part, not making a joke of it. Certainly, the wrong done in this world can seem

---

[17] Ibid., 1.

[18] Ibid., 2.

overwhelming at times. Sometimes, this leads us to make light of evil in an effort, conscious or subconscious, to disarm it or cope with it. We should be careful about this response. Ephesians 5:4 warns against inappropriate joking or foolish talk. It suggests this behavior can, since it is not reproof, imply acceptance of or sharing in such evil deeds (v. 11), since "it is a shame even to speak of those things which are done of them in secret" (v. 12). Evil is not funny. It is abhorrent. Christians caught up in evil behavior need to be confronted so that they can be rescued. Making them the butt of jokes denies the seriousness of their evil, our desire for their good, or both.

"Cast the Speck Out"

Abhorring evil also means confronting it in our lives and the lives of others. We have already discussed rebuking, but rebuking usually involves addressing a sin which has been committed against us. The sort of confrontation we have in mind here is in some ways more difficult for it is not "minding our own business." It is going to one's brother to pluck the mote out of his eye. And, since this is a touchy subject at best, it is helpful to review Jesus' words from Matthew 7.

Matthew 7 begins, "Judge not, lest you be judged." These words have been thrown up many times against the believer who sought to address evil behavior. As often as not, they are thrown up by the believer himself in his own mind, whether out of sincere concern or just to avoid the painful responsibility love places upon him. However, what Jesus says next makes clear that these words are far from a prohibition against confrontation. He goes on:

> Why do you see the speck that is in thy brother's eye, but do not attend to the beam that is in your eye? Or, how will you say to your brother, Let me cast the speck out of your eye; and, behold, the beam is in your eye? Hypocrite! First, cast the beam out of your eye; and then you will see clearly to cast the speck out of your brother's eye (Matt 7:3-5).

There is a command here to confront the reality of the grit in your brother's eye. It is the way this confrontation is done that distinguishes it from the judgment Jesus prohibits.

First, the approach begins with a humble recognition that we too have evil in our hearts we must abhor. We confront the evil in the lives of our fellow believers because we are like them, not because we are different. The specific way our evils manifest themselves may differ, but they have more in common than they differ from one another.

Second, the approach is to bring health and healing to the brother, not condemnation. The approach is not, "You have glass in your eye and I hope it cuts your eye and you get infected and die." It is an approach which desires one thing, that the speck be removed from the eye so that good will follow. That is, it desires that the evil behavior leave the life of one's brother so that his life will be good, beneficial, for him.

Third, the approach recognizes that the evil in a Christian life, whether his or ours, does not belong there. This is not talking about confronting a non-Christian. To be blunt, evil is the only thing one will find in the life of a lost person. A life lived at enmity with God is a life devoid of true, unmixed good. But a Christian life should be otherwise. And the way we confront those who claim the name of Christ should reflect that expectation. We abhor evil in the life of a Christian precisely because it does not belong there. And we cannot ignore such evil, again, because it does not belong there.

One might say, We live in a fallen world and, as long as we are in this life, we will struggle with sin. This is true, but this does not change the fact that evil does not belong in our lives as Christians. Consider a man who stumbles into a town after crossing the desert during a sandstorm. We might expect that he will have gotten some grit in his eyes. Do we leave it in there because we expect it to be there? Of course not. That we expect to find evil in our own hearts moves us to examine ourselves to cast it out. Failing to do so makes us the hypocrite Jesus warns against. But, knowing the evil in our own hearts also moves us to look for the evil in our brother that is hurting him. And we look for it to help him remove it.

"Do not Cast Your Pearls before Swine"

None of this is to suggest that it is the Christian's job to openly, immediately, and directly confront every instance of behavior which the Bible deems evil. These are instructions about how to abhor evil among brothers, not requirements about how to treat "dogs" or "swine," how Jesus metaphorically speaks of those who have not yet been sanctified by trusting in him (Matt 7:6). But our lives should reflect an abhorrence of evil. We do not pretend it is good or go along with those who do. We do not consider it something to make light of or joke about. When we find it in the eyes of a brother, we confront him to help him remove it. We love people. Evil hurts people. We abhor evil.

Reflection Questions

1. Do you tend to think of the things the Bible calls evil as primarily displeasing God or harmful to people? How does this affect how you approach those things?

2. Why is our world so willing to confront some things that are potentially harmful to people, such as smoking, but so unwilling to confront others?

3. In terms of love, what does it mean that people, as a whole, are so willing and so prone to do things that are not in our best interests? What does it mean when we do not do anything about it?

"Love Is . . ."

There are many things that could be said about what it means for Christians to love and how Christians should put love into practice. But every text must end at some point, and this one has sought to reflect on some of the key principles which this author believes are neglected among Christians today. In this concluding chapter, we shall consider the "Love Chapter" of 1 Corinthians, 1 Corinthians 13. In vv. 4-8, Paul reflects on love in terms of what it is, what it is not, and what it does. Considering his words makes a fitting end to our discussion.

Paul begins by mentioning two positive traits of love, by which he means behaviors of people who do love. People who love are longsuffering and kind. Longsuffering in Scripture usually refers to being patient with people rather than responding to their failings and sins with wrath or judgment. In Romans, Paul speaks of God being longsuffering, in that He does not immediately destroy the wicked for their sins (2:4, 9:22). Peter uses it in a similar manner, using it to describe God waiting to send the judgment of the Flood while Noah built the ark (1 Peter 3:20). Kindness similarly is connected to dealing easily with people, particularly those who are difficult to put up with.[19] The loving person puts up with people at their

---

[19] An adjective related to this verb is used, for example, to describe how God deals with the thankless in Luke 6:35.

worst. This makes sense; it rarely takes love to put up with people at their best.

That these two words, longsuffering and kindness, are all Paul says about the positive character of love is a reminder that biblical love often is not what we have in mind when we think of love on an everyday basis. The young man who thinks, "Man, I love that girl," sitting next to the young lady probably has other positive things in mind. His list would be more like:

Love is exciting.
Love is fun.
Love laughs and smiles.
Love gets goosebumps.
Love stays out late.

And this is how it should be. He might not be sitting next to her much longer if he ended an evening with, "Sweetie, I really suffered long tonight." But biblical love, the love God commands us to have for one another, is not about the good times. It is not about the laughs and the smiles. It kicks in when that sort of love is pushed past its limit.

Paul then shifts to negative features of love, things love, that is, the one who loves, does not do. The first of these is that love does not envy. This is language used of Joseph's brothers in Acts 7:9 to refer to their jealousy over Jacob's preference of Joseph. It is used of the Jews in Acts 13:45 to refer to their unwillingness to allow "the whole city," including Gentiles, to hear the message they thought was theirs. Envy thus seems to refer to anger at the one loved over good that loved one experiences. A Christian cannot, if he loves, look at another Christian and be angry or upset about good that comes to that other Christian. This is the case even, indeed especially, when that is good which you believe should be yours. Is the nearby church booming? Did your fellow Christian get a job you applied for? Did she get a car just like the one you just bought, and at a better price? Love does not envy those things. It is not troubled at them; indeed, it should rejoice in them.

On the other hand, it is an error to understand this envy as "jealousy," as it is sometimes translated. Jealousy in contemporary English usually refers to the passionate guarding of exclusive relationships. God is clear that such jealousy is often appropriate; He is jealous Himself, as He and His prophets say seven times (Exod 20:5, 34:14; Deut 4:24, 5:9, 6:15; Josh 24:19; Nah 1:2), and considers His relationship with His people to be exclusive. There is nothing unloving about guarding such relationships.

Next, love is not prideful. This is expressed in two ways, that it does not vaunt itself and is not puffed up. This is an expectation of Christian behavior that is commonly expressed because it is a constant concern. The one who loves does not put himself first. He does not think of himself as higher than those around him and thus worthy of better treatment or better outcomes. Even if he is faithfully obeying God and living a flawless life, he does not begin to think of himself as deserving high treatment. Jesus expressed this idea well in Luke 17:7-10. There he asks whether a man with a servant working in the field will thank him for his work and fix him dinner. He says, Of course not. So we, Christ's followers, when we have done all he commands, should say, "We are unprofitable servants. We have done that which was our duty to do." It is interesting that this word "unprofitable" appears only one other place in the New Testament, in Matt 25:30, where it is used to describe a servant cast into outer darkness. The Christian loves by remembering that he himself was saved from damnation solely by the grace of God. He does not think of himself higher than that.[20]

Love does not seek its own. As we have discussed already, love seeks the good of others. This verse emphasizes that this is all it does. Love is never about seeking one's own good. There is no negotiation here. When we find ourselves weighing our good against that of another and trying to balance the two, we fall short of truly loving.

Alexis de Tocqueville notes in his *Democracy in America* that the Christians he encountered in early America considered serving their fellow man part of their own self-interest. They believed this because they believed that God would reward them in glory. Yet de Tocqueville expresses disbelief:

> Nevertheless I cannot believe that all those who practise virtue from religious motives are only actuated by the hope of a recompense. I have known zealous Christians who constantly forgot themselves, to work with greater ardor for the happiness of their fellow-men; and I have heard them declare that all they did was only to earn the blessings of a future state. I cannot but think that they deceive themselves; I respect them too much to believe

---

[20]The next clause, that love does not behave itself unseemly, contains language that is too rare to explicate confidently beyond the basic translation.

them.[21]

This is an important point. It is the truth that Christians who love will find various positives to doing so. Aside from rewards from God, they may find enjoyment and satisfaction in their deeds. But finding pleasure in good deeds is not necessarily the same as seeking one's own in them. At the same time, true love put into practice will be like what de Toqueville saw. Those who practice it may be confident of the rewards for it, but those are not truly their motivations for the practice.

These words, that love does not seek its own, also should not be taken to mean that the lover should make absolutely clear he is not seeking his own by pointing out how much he does not like, does not benefit from, or does not prefer what he is doing. Much as Jesus warned against looking like one is fasting so everyone will know, Christians should be careful about looking like they are loving (Matt 6:16-18). Such behavior in fact amounts to seeking one's own. It asks either for recognition of how loving one is being or relief from having to love when others see how miserable a certain activity makes one. Imagine if your neighbor helped you with a task, such as cutting down some trees in your yard. Afterwards, you thank him. He responds, "You are welcome. I hated doing it. I don't like chainsaws. That bark was scratchy. It was pretty hot today and now I am all sweaty," and so on. How welcome

---

[21] Alexis de Tocqueville, *Democracy in America*, trans. Henry Reeve, 2.2.9.

do you really think you are, from all that? How likely are you to ask for help, any sort of help, again?

Love is not provoked. The language here is uncommon in the New Testament, appearing only here and in Acts 17:16, when the idolatry of Athens stirs Paul to action. If we presume that Paul's response in Acts 17 is proper, his point cannot be that a loving person cannot be provoked to act in a certain way. Instead, he is saying that love itself does not come and go based upon passions or fleeting circumstances. Biblical love is not something we feel at one moment and lose the next. It is constant, reliable, and consistent. As Warren Barfield sings, love is "a house we enter in and then commit to never leave."[22] The love within us may be provoked to take certain actions, but the love itself should be a stable ground from which all our responses stem.

Love does not think evil. Instead, love thinks the best of those loved. Much of the time, our relationships with other people are governed in large part by the mental constructs into which we press their actions. For example, if someone does not show up for an appointment, our response is determined in part by the reason. You might be angry if you thought he just forgot or she just stood you up. On the other hand, no one could be angry at someone who was late because his car was hit by a train. It is easy, when someone acts in a way that hurts or distresses us, to interpret their actions in the worst possible light. This is especially true when the action is one that we

---

[22] Warren Barfield, "Love Is Not a Fight," by Warren Barfield, *Love Is Not a Fight,* Provident Label Group, 2007, CD.

ourselves would only do if we meant to be hurtful. Here is, again, where we need to remember that love inverts standards. I have already mentioned my appreciation for manners. Had I ever called one of my professors by first name, I would have meant to be rude. However, I should not think such evil of a student who does not call me, "Dr." He may be completely innocent in his heart and mean no offense. There are actions God deems wrong that are thus certainly wrong, but there are many actions that are only morally wrong if we think of evil motives behind them. Love does not do that.

Love does not rejoice in iniquity, but rejoices in truth. Here, again, love's close relationship to the truth and its abhorrence of evil is stated. These were developed in past chapters, so we will not belabor them here.

Love bears, believes, hopes, and endures all things. Here, Paul presents love as a source of endless resources. As we deal with people in loving ways, there are always times when we want to say, Enough. I've had enough of that. I can't believe him anymore. She'll never change. But love does not do that. It always has more to offer. And thus, as Paul concludes, love never fails.

Here Paul uses language with a double meaning as he transitions from discussing love as an aspect of the life of a believer to the place of love in the eternal divine plan. In the life of a believer, true love never fails. This does not mean, as we have discussed previously, that it always achieves its desired particular end; some people may resist love until the end. But when Christians truly desire the good of others with such sincerity that they will do anything at their own expense to bring about that good, they cannot fail to distinguish themselves as followers of Christ. In the divine plan, love never ends. There are aspects of the divine plan which are limited to this life. Faith that is not based on literal physical sight ends when we see Christ as he is. Hope for a resurrected body ends when we receive that resurrected body. But love is not like these. Even when we are enjoying eternal bliss with God and the rest of His people in His glory, there will still be love. There will still be a desire, now unhindered by fallenness, sin, or mortal weakness, for the good of others that would lead, were it necessary, for us to sacrifice to bring about that good. God will still love His people that way, and His people will still love that way. Loving now is, in this sense, making the present look like eternity. And it is to this that Christians are called. May we all do so.

Reflection Questions

1. What can you do this week to love that, maybe, you should have been doing already?

2. Is it difficult for you to distinguish between love that takes pleasure in the presence of another person and love that suffers long in the presence of another person? Is it difficult to call both of those love? Why is that?

3. In eternity, there will be love even though there will be no needs to be met of the sort we face now. What does this say about of what love really consists?

Bibliography

Arkowitz, Hal and Scott O. Lilienfeld. "Is Divorce Bad for Children?" http://www.scientificamerican.com/article/is-divorce-bad-for-children, accessed Apr 1, 2016.

Barfield, Warren. "Love Is Not a Fight," by Warren Barfield. *Love Is Not a Fight.* Provident Label Group, 2007. CD.

Center for Disease Control. *Sexual Identiy, Sex of Sexual Contacts, and Helath-Risk Behaviors Among Students in Grades 9-12 – Youth Risk Behavior Surveillance, Selected Sites, United States, 2001-2009* .

de Tocqueville, Alexis. *Democracy in America.* 2 vols. Translated by Henry Reeve. New York: George Dearborn and Co., 1835-1840.

Fletcher, Joseph. *Situation Ethics.* Philadelphia: Westminster, 1966.

Sailhamer, John. *The Pentateuch as Narrative: A Biblical-Theological Commentary.* Grand Rapids: Zondervan, 1992.

Made in the USA
San Bernardino, CA
24 January 2019